Which A levels?

The guide to choosing
A levels and other post-16 qualifications

Alison Dixon

Which A levels?

The guide to choosing A levels and other post-16 qualifications

Ninth edition

Published by Honeyman Publishing 2016

honeymanpublishing@gmail.com

© Alison Dixon

www.alisondixon.co.uk

ISBN 978-1-326-57358-4

Cover design by Andy Southan, Wordcraft Typesetting

Typesetting by Wordcraft Typesetting (01483 560735)

In memory of

Professor Sir Harry Kroto
Nobel Laureate in chemistry

1939 – 2016

whose boundless enthusiasm inspired so many young people in their careers.

Acknowledgements

With thanks to Alan Whicheloe, Andy Southan,
Helen Evans and Margaret Kroto.

CONTENTS

A level subjects

YOUR POST-16 OPTIONS

The next two years

When you complete your GCSEs, or equivalent, you must choose your next step. You might want to continue studying at school, or go to a different sixth form or college. You also have the option to continue your learning part time through an apprenticeship or a job with training.

Your choice of qualifications

Many people who decide to continue studying after GCSEs opt for A levels. This book provides detailed information on A levels, including descriptions of over 30 A level subjects and where each could lead. However, remember that there are alternative qualifications at the same level (Level 3) such as BTEC National qualifications or Cambridge Technicals. It is possible to combine these qualifications alongside A levels, so your choice of qualifications is wide.

Tech levels

Technical level qualifications (tech levels) are for 16-year-old students who have a clear idea about the occupation they wish to pursue. They are vocational and equip students with the specialist knowledge they need for a specific recognised occupation, such as engineering, computing, accounting or hospitality.

Raising the Participation Age

Besides continuing with full-time study after 16, your other options include apprenticeships or paid work or voluntary work that must including training. In England you must undertake training because of legislation known as Raising the Participation Age or RPA. Any young person now has to stay in 'education and training' until the end of the academic year they turn 18.

Apprenticeships

Apprenticeships have been popular in countries like Germany and Switzerland for many years and are recognised routes into many professions. In the UK, although a valid and successful route in years gone by, they have taken a while to become established as an alternative to higher education. They are now gaining in popularity as people realise how they can boost career chances in a challenging economy as well as being a cost-effective way of obtaining qualifications, even up to degree level.

Apprenticeships are available in many career areas. They are offered at different levels:
- Intermediate Level Apprenticeships – equivalent to GCSE level (Level 2)
- Advanced Level Apprenticeships – equivalent to A level or BTEC National (Level 3)
- Higher Apprenticeships – equivalent to a Level 4 qualification or higher (Level 5/6)
- Degree Apprenticeships – equivalent to a Level 6/7 qualification.

Apprenticeships are a realistic alternative to studying full time. Higher Apprenticeships and Degree Apprenticeships offer progression to higher education.

Higher Apprenticeships

Higher Apprenticeships are an alternative to higher education as more companies, including major employers such as Rolls Royce, BT and PWC, run these programmes. Apprentices work towards qualifications at higher education level, gain valuable work experience and skills for their CV, and get paid at the same time.

Higher Apprenticeships normally require A levels or equivalent for entry, so they are the obvious route after sixth form. Some of them will express their offers as UCAS points. They involve a combination of learning on the job, working alongside experienced colleagues, with off-the-job training at a college, university or perhaps a company training centre. Many Higher Apprenticeships offer the opportunity to study towards a foundation degree, HND or honours degree. There may also be the opportunity to work towards professional qualifications specific to an industry - for example, engineers can take the first steps towards gaining chartered status.

Degree Apprenticeships

These are apprenticeships where study for a degree is an integral part of the programme. They are currently available in aerospace engineering, aerospace software development, automotive engineering, banking relationship manager, chartered surveying, construction, defence systems engineering, digital, electronic systems engineering, laboratory science, nuclear, power systems, public relations, food engineering, food science and dairy technology.

Degree apprentices split their time between university study and the workplace and are employed throughout – gaining a full bachelors or masters degree while earning a wage and getting on-the-job experience. Higher apprentices are already able study to degree level as part of their apprenticeship but Degree Apprenticeships go further. They involve a degree as an integral part of the apprenticeship, co-designed by employers to make sure it is relevant for the skills industry is looking for.

See https://www.gov.uk/apply-apprenticeship for details of the National Apprenticeship Service where you can search online for vacancies. In Wales you can search on www.careerswales.com

Work now, study later?

Some people decide to have a break in full-time education and then resume their studies as a mature student. Many students also consider a gap year between completing their sixth form study and higher education. Gap years can consist of anything from work (paid or voluntary) to travel, or a mixture of both. In general, admissions officers in higher education are positive about gap years as they feel that students benefit from increased experience and maturity.

However, for some subjects, such as mathematics, where a break may affect progress, or for longer courses, such as medicine, it is always advisable to check with admissions tutors for their advice.

What to do next

The decision is yours and yours alone. Help and advice are available from your careers teacher or careers adviser in school or college.

You will need to consider all the alternatives and all the issues surrounding A levels and other post-16 options. Parents and friends can also offer advice, although they may not have the latest information.

To help you to decide, ask yourself some basic questions:

- Why am I interested in studying further?
- Would I benefit from further study?
- Would I learn better through a mixture of work and training?
- Do I really understand what is involved in further study?
- Do my teachers think I am right to continue in full-time education?
- Do I know what is available?
- What am I good at (including skills and knowledge outside the classroom)?
- What do I really enjoy?
- What would I do after further study? Go on to university or college, or into an apprenticeship/job that includes further training?
- Do I have any clear ideas about a career or the future?

HIGHER EDUCATION

What is it and how do I decide whether it is for me?

Higher education does not just mean going to university. Higher education courses can also be taken at a college of higher or further education or studied by distance learning (including via the internet) and can be part time as well as full time. You can study locally or in another part of the country. Your course might last anything from two to five years and could include work or study placements in the UK or worldwide. Your higher education could form part of a Higher or Degree Apprenticeship.

What courses are available?

➤ **Degree courses**: these are courses that people automatically think about when they are thinking of higher education. They usually last three or four years, full time (longer if you are studying a subject such as medicine). They can also be studied part time whilst working, as in an apprenticeship.

➤ **HNC/HND courses**: Higher National Certificates (HNCs) and Diplomas (HNDs) are work-related qualifications, available in everything from accounting to film production. HNCs are the part-time alternative to HNDs. Students often study an HNC part time over two years, while they are in employment.

HNDs take two years to complete on a full-time basis (or three years with a work placement). HNCs and HNDs can allow entry into the second or third year of a degree course if you do well.

➤ **Foundation degrees**: these are qualifications designed with the involvement of employers, and combine academic study with developing workplace skills. Some have been designed to tackle particular skills shortages. They last two years, full time (or they can be taken part time) and it's possible to progress to further or higher study or top up to a full degree. You may go straight into work after a foundation degree. You can search for foundation degree courses on the UCAS website.

Art Foundation course

If you are thinking of studying art and design at university, you usually have to study an Art Foundation course at a college of further education or art school, then move on to your degree studies. Entry to college or art school depends far more on a strong portfolio (collection of artwork that you have produced) than specified grades for A levels or equivalent.

A LEVELS

If you are considering taking A levels, think about some of these questions:
- Do I know the full range of options at 16+?
- Why do I want to do A levels?
- How demanding are A levels?
- How can I do well at them?
- What subjects should I study?
- Should I study at school or college?
- Have I taken advice from careers advisers, teachers, parents and friends?

The new A levels

A level specifications are being revised and revised subjects are gradually being phased in. The new A levels will be awarded with the same A* to E grades as previously used.

New A levels in England

The 'new' AS levels are now a separate qualification and no longer count towards the A level grade. It will still be a one-year course with exams at the end. Assessment will be mostly through exams although in some cases there may be a limited amount of coursework. The new AS level will be worth 40% of the UCAS points of an A level whereas an 'old' AS will continue to be worth 50%.

New A levels in England are linear rather than modular, which means exams take place at the end of the two-year course, rather than assessment after each module. There may be some coursework, depending on the subject. Note that the new linear A levels will only operate in England.

What does this mean for you?

This means that some students will end up studying a mixture of 'old' and 'new' A levels if they are taking subjects that have not yet been revised. Many schools and colleges will still offer the opportunity to take the AS level exam at the end of the first year.

This is because:
- universities have made it very clear that they will continue to use students' AS grades when considering their applications and
- students will still need to show they are performing well enough at AS level in order to be allowed to progress to second year A level study.

How universities have responded to the changes

Universities are considering how they will respond to the changes in AS and A level qualifications, especially as different schools and colleges might have different approaches, with some only offering A levels and some offering both AS and A levels. Therefore, for entry to university from now on you should check with universities that are of interest to you.

Choosing your A level subjects

The two most important criteria for choosing subjects are:
- what you are likely to be good at and
- what you are likely to enjoy.

You will find there are some subjects available that you won't have come across previously at school. Find out about them before you choose. The subjects listed in this book will be a good place to start.

Most higher education courses require certain A level grades (or alternative equivalent qualifications), and many specify the A level subjects and GCSE subjects that you should have. Think ahead to what you will be doing after A levels to help you choose the best subjects now. If you are not sure what career you will enter, try to choose a selection of subjects that will keep your options as open as possible.

Therefore, when making your choices you should consider:
- the subjects in which you are interested
- your abilities, aptitudes and skills
- how open you want to keep your career choice
- which A level subjects are available at your school or in local sixth forms and colleges.

A level subject combinations

Some A levels cover common ground, for example, geography and environmental science, or business and economics. If the overlap is too great, some higher education institutions may not accept the combination as counting as two separate A level subjects for admissions purposes. On the other hand, two complementary subjects may help a great deal in your studies. For example, doing physics without mathematics or another science would be difficult and is not generally recommended.

Some degree courses specify the A level subjects that you need. The following list shows the most popular degrees that often require specific A levels:

➤ **Architecture** – often a mix of arts and sciences, sometimes maths and physics required, sometimes a design portfolio

➤ **Biology** – biology, often chemistry or another science or maths

➤ **Chemistry** – chemistry and sometimes maths and/or another science

➤ **Computer science** – some courses required maths

➤ **Dentistry** – chemistry, often biology and one or two other sciences or maths

➤ **Engineering** – maths and physics (or maths and chemistry for chemical engineering)

➤ **Maths** – maths and possibly further maths

➤ **Medicine** – chemistry and usually one or two other sciences. A choice of chemistry and biology and one from maths and physics satisfies all UK medical school requirements. For candidates without science subjects at A level or equivalent, it is possible to undertake an additional pre-medical year at some universities. The pre-medical year is a preliminary course in chemistry, physics and biology.

➤ **Modern languages** – usually you will need the language at A level but requirements vary, especially for less common languages

➤ **Music** – music; performing courses will ask for a certain standard of performance such as Grade VIII

➤ **Physics** – physics and maths

➤ **Veterinary science** – chemistry, biology and maths satisfy all veterinary school requirements. Other sciences may be considered.

Facilitating subjects

Some courses at universities require applicants to have studied certain subjects already, so you must be sure how your choices at school and college may close off certain subjects at university. A group of universities called the Russell Group has listed subjects that are usually considered by universities to be helpful and/or required at advanced level (e.g. A level) for particular courses.

These subjects are called 'facilitating' because choosing them at advanced level leaves open a wide range of options for university study. These facilitating subjects are maths and further maths, physics, biology, chemistry, history, geography, modern and classical languages and English literature. For more information see www.russellgroup.ac.uk

Core Maths

Core Maths is an exam that you can take alongside your A levels. It has been designed to maintain and develop real-life maths skills. You don't study just theory, you study maths that can be applied on a day-to-day basis in work, study or everyday life and most courses will include a financial maths element. It will also help with other A level subjects, in particular with science, geography, business, psychology and economics.

It has been developed so that students keep up their maths skills after GCSE as maths skills are becoming increasingly important in the workplace and in higher education. Many students who study maths after GCSE improve their career choices and increase their earning potential. It is a Level 3 qualification that attracts UCAS points.

Alternatives to A levels

There is a range of qualifications that you could consider instead of, or in combination with, A levels. Some of these qualifications, such as BTEC National and Cambridge Technical qualifications, are widely available. Other programmes of learning included below, such as the International Baccalaureate or Cambridge Pre-U, are offered by some institutions.

BTEC National qualifications

These are specialist vocational qualifications useful for entry to employment and higher education. They focus on applied knowledge and understanding of a specialised area. BTEC National qualifications are practical, work-related courses and are at level 3, the same level as A levels. You learn by completing projects and assignments that are based on realistic workplace situations, activities and demands. Students focus on a particular subject area and develop a range of specialist skills and knowledge. BTEC qualifications attract points on the UCAS tariff. Apart from the BTEC Diploma, which is the equivalent of two full A levels, there is an Extended BTEC Diploma, equivalent to three full A levels. They are worth considering as they may suit your learning style more than A levels.

Here are some examples of the areas in which you can take a BTEC Diploma (and there are many others): animal management, applied science, art and design, business, children's play, learning and development, computing, engineering, enterprise and entrepreneurship, health and social care, information technology, music, music technology, performing arts, retail, sport, sport and exercise science.

To find out more about these and other subjects go to the Edexcel website: www.edexcel.org.uk

Cambridge Technicals

Cambridge Technicals are vocational qualifications at Level 2 and Level 3. They're designed for the workplace and are an alternative to A levels.

The qualifications allow for a high degree of flexibility with the choice of units that make up the qualifications, so students can specialise in the specific areas of the subject that interest them most. The Level 3 Cambridge Technicals attract UCAS points and can be used for entry to university as well as employment

They are available many subject areas including: art and design, business, digital media, engineering, health and social care, IT, laboratory skills, media and communication, performing arts, sports and physical activity.

For further information go to the OCR website: www.ocr.org.uk

International Baccalaureate (IB)

The International Baccalaureate Diploma programme is equivalent to other post-16 qualifications, such as A levels. It normally takes two years and covers a broader range of subjects than A levels. You study six subjects, which include mathematics, your own language, a foreign language, a humanities subject, a science and an arts subject. You could take a second foreign language or science in place of the arts subject. The IB Diploma also includes an extended essay. The IB Diploma is accepted for university entry and attracts points on the UCAS tariff. To find out more see www.ibo.org

Cambridge Pre-U

The Cambridge Pre-U is an alternative to A levels. It aims to prepare students with the skills and knowledge they need to be successful in higher education and attracts UCAS points. It consists of 25 principal subjects plus the core Global Perspectives and Research (GPR) element.

The Cambridge Pre-U Diploma is awarded to those completing three principal subjects and the core GPR component. Up to two A levels may be substituted for the principal subjects. The Cambridge Pre-U GPR element can be taken as a freestanding package, and a separate qualification. You can find out more at www.cie.org.uk

AQA Bacc

This consists of three A levels plus an AS level or Level 3 Core Maths qualification. It also includes an Extended Project Qualification (EPQ) and core enrichment activities, which include work-related learning, community or voluntary work and personal development activities such as public speaking, first aid, photography, sport or performing arts. See www.aqa.org.uk for more information.

Welsh Baccalaureate

The Welsh Baccalaureate Diploma is formed of two parts and was revised in 2015.

Skills Challenge Certificate – this is to enable students to develop and demonstrate an understanding of, and proficiency in, essential and employability skills: communication, numeracy, digital literacy, planning and organisation, creativity and innovation, critical thinking and problem solving, and personal effectiveness. You work on three challenges: Enterprise and Employability, Global Citizenship and Community plus an individual project.

Supporting qualifications – consists of qualifications such as GCSEs, maths and numeracy, AS/A levels and BTECs.

The Welsh Baccalaureate Diploma is available at four levels; Advanced, National (post 16), Foundation (post 16) and National/Foundation (KS4). The Advanced Diploma is accepted for entry into higher education and apprenticeships and attracts UCAS points. For more information, visit www.welshbaccalaureate.org.uk

Scottish Highers and Advanced Highers

Available in Scotland, Highers are the qualifications usually needed for entry into university or college to study for degrees and Higher National courses (HNCs and HNDs).

Four or five Highers are normally taken in Scotland in the fifth and sixth year of secondary school or at a college of further education and are studied in considerable depth, involving coursework and final examinations. Advanced Highers are taken in the sixth year at school, or at college, and are aimed particularly at students who have passed Highers. They extend the skills and knowledge gained at Higher level and are additional qualifications that are useful for entry into higher education or the workplace. Universities express their entry requirements in terms of Highers; entry profiles for Highers and Advanced Highers can be found on the UCAS website, www.ucas.com

Scottish Baccalaureate

There are four, available in languages, science, expressive arts or social sciences.

They consist of a group of relevant Higher and Advanced Higher qualifications depending on the area chosen. In addition there is an Interdisciplinary Project. This is an Advanced Higher Unit in which you apply your subject knowledge in realistic contexts. The Interdisciplinary Project helps students develop and show evidence of initiative, responsibility and independent working – skills useful for further study and/or employment. Find out more at www.sqa.org.uk/baccalaureates

ACCOUNTING

Accountancy studies the money side of business and will help you gain an understanding of the wider business environment, how financial control is vital to business success and how, without it, even profitable firms can fail. You will learn about the effects of economic, legal and technological change on accounting, and the social implications of accounting decisions. You will also learn valuable accounting and reporting skills.

The new specifications encourage you to 'think like an accountant'. You will analyse, use and evaluate projects, and prepare financial statements for businesses, even those with incomplete records. You will be involved in preparing information to enable managers to plan, control and make decisions using a range of different accounting techniques. You will be taught to apply your knowledge of accounting theory and practice to develop commercial acumen and financial awareness. You will learn how to work ethically and professionally.

An interest in business and GCSE maths will be an advantage and may be an entry requirement. You don't need any experience in accounting as the A/AS level can be started from scratch.

What do you study?

The topics listed give an idea of what could be covered. The exact content of specifications differs according to exam boards. You will need to check with your school or college about the exact options available to you.

There are two main types of business accounting which are covered by the A level:

Financial accounting: mainly concerned with the current state of a company's accounts. Financial accountants undertake auditing (checking in detail) the financial records of companies and preparing annual accounts for HM Revenue & Customs and shareholders.

Management accounting: mainly deals with examining a company's accounts to help senior managers plan and make decisions. As you progress through your course, you are often put in the role of financial adviser to the managers of a business. You are asked to recommend the actions that the business should take to improve its performance or to get out of financial trouble.

Financial accounting

➢ **Accounting records** – how to keep records of a company's financial activity, including the double-entry model (every credit on one account must be

1

matched by a debit on another), how to treat debts, creditors, investments and capital. You will be required to apply your technical understanding of the double entry accounting model in the preparation of financial statements for a range of business organisations.

➤ **Formal presentation of financial information** – trial balances, cash-flow statements, balance sheets, profit-and-loss accounts and published company accounts. Preparing financial statements for sole traders as well as limited companies.

➤ **Stock valuation** – how to organise and present information about stock held by a business organisation.

Management accounting

➤ **Budgeting and cash-flow forecasts** – predicting the company's financial future and how these are used in future planning. Analysing and evaluating business performance.

➤ **Break-even analysis** – assessing whether a business project can cover its costs and how much it must sell before making a profit.

➤ **Capital investment appraisal** – the pros and cons of investing money.

➤ **Overheads** – accounting for indirect costs that are not incurred in the actual product or a service (e.g. an IT system).

➤ **Analysing and evaluation of financial information** – understanding what accounts can (and can't) tell you about the health and prospects of a business, and using ratios to analyse business performance.

➤ **Planning, control and decision making** – how decisions are made on the basis of financial information and how managers use this to plan ahead.

You will also cover:

➤ **an introduction to the role of the accountant in business** – finding out about the responsibilities of the accountant within business, the difference between financial accounting and management accounting and the purpose of each. The role of the accountant in developing and overseeing accounting information systems to provide reliable and relevant information for both financial and management purposes.

➤ **types of business organisation** – learning about different types of business organisations including different business ownership models, the associated benefits and risks and the impact on financial reporting. This will include sole traders, partnerships and limited liability companies. Also the sources of finance for different forms of business organisation and the risks related to these.

➢ **ethical considerations** – principles of ethical behaviour including integrity, objectivity, professional competence and due care, confidentially and professional behaviour. Legal and regulation requirements in the accounting sector and the importance of working within these requirements. What to do if there is a suspicion that an unethical or illegal act has been committed.

➢ **presentation and communication** – presenting accounting information in different formats so that it can be understood by non-accountants and so can be used by them for decision making.

The new specifications concentrate on qualitative and quantitative skills and these will form 20% of the A level examination. There is no coursework requirement.

Subject combinations

Popular A level combinations include business, economics, computer science, languages and law. A Core Maths qualification might be helpful but is not a substitute for maths A level if that is required for a degree course. Make sure there isn't too much overlap with other subjects, especially business studies. If you are considering accountancy at degree level, some universities ask for mathematics or statistics at A level.

Accounting A level is not a requirement for accountancy courses, and while some courses find it a useful preparation others may not accept it. Check with higher education institutions.

GCSE maths is an essential requirement as is English.

Higher education options

Degree-level study

You don't need an accountancy degree to qualify as an accountant so you could consider related subjects such as business studies, maths, economics, actuarial science or law. Quantity surveying is another option, as quantity surveyors are the accountants of the construction industry.

To qualify as a professional accountant after graduating, you will need to undertake further training and study part time for professional exams. An accountancy degree can offer exemptions from some of these exams. Some other degree subjects, such as business and management, business economics, business information technology and management science, also give exemptions. Check with professional accountancy bodies for a full list.

Many degrees are called 'accounting and finance', but have the same content as 'accounting' or 'accountancy'. Some degrees have an international perspective, including languages and a period of study or work abroad.

Degree subject combinations

Accounting can be combined with many subjects. ICT, economics, law, marketing, business studies and psychology are popular, but if you reduce the proportion of accountancy in your degree you may not get all the professional exam exemptions.

Other higher education qualifications

There are foundation degrees available in accounting, business and financial management and accounting and finance. Accounting, business accounting and related subjects such as business and management are available at HND/HNC. You will need to check to see if they give any exemptions from professional accountancy exams.

Relevance to other subjects?

Your accounting A level is useful even if you don't intend to qualify as an accountant or work in business. The understanding you gain of business and finance is useful for degree courses in business, economics, law, IT, marketing, administration or tourism amongst many others.

Important advice

If you are considering a year out between A levels and your degree, check with the institutions. Some prefer accountancy students not to take gap years, or ask that you get some relevant work experience. Make your plans clear on your UCAS application.

Future careers

After A levels

Higher Apprenticeships are available in accounting which combine work experience with university-level study. The professional services Higher Apprenticeship offers training pathways in audit, tax, management consulting and management accounting. CIPFA run their own finance apprenticeship scheme and require 3 A levels.

The ICAEW (Institute of Chartered Accountants in England and Wales) offers a training route with qualifications from the Association of Accounting Technicians (AAT). This is a fast-track route, which enables you to qualify as a chartered accountant in four years. Employers usually ask for between 240 and 320 UCAS points (or 96 to 128 points under the new UCAS Tariff).

To qualify as a chartered accountant without a degree involves a four-year training contract with a firm of chartered accountants or with a company finance department. During this time you would take AAT and ICAEW exams. You then join graduate entrants to the profession as you move on to the professional training stage. The route to qualification with the other professional bodies is very similar.

You could consider qualifying as an accounting technician and may get some exemptions for the qualification because of your A level in accounting. The course is based on skills tests and simulations and training is offered by the AAT and the Association of Chartered Certified Accountants (ACCA).

If you don't plan to qualify as an accountant, there are opportunities for working in finance departments of many organisations. Such jobs involve arranging salaries, paying bills and issuing invoices. A management trainee scheme or apprenticeship would allow you to use your accounting skills and undertake further training.

You could consider working in banks or building societies, or becoming a financial adviser.

Skills gained like numeracy, research and analysis, problem-solving, communication and computer skills will be useful in many jobs.

After a degree

Working in accounting

Below are the areas of accountancy open to graduates. The choice of professional body that you train with depends on the kind of work you want to do.

➢   **Chartered accountants** work in private practice mainly dealing with taxation and auditing. Chartered accountancy firms mainly operate as partners, so if you become a partner, you take a share of the profits rather than a salary. Private practice accountants usually qualify with the ICAEW.

➤ **Certified accountants** work as salaried employees in commerce or industry. In all but the smallest businesses, they have either a financial or management accountancy role. The professional body for this type of accountancy is the ACCA, but ICAEW and ACCA qualifications are interchangeable.

➤ **Management accountants** are more firmly oriented towards business, especially financial planning and strategy, and the use of IT for management information. They qualify with the Chartered Institute of Management Accountants (CIMA).

➤ **Public finance accountants** work within the Civil Service, NHS or local government. Public service has a very clear career structure but is a specialised form of accounting so it might be difficult to move into other areas. Public finance accountants qualify with the Chartered Institute of Public Finance and Accountancy (CIPFA).

➤ **Accounting technicians** work alongside professionally qualified accountants collecting financial information to assist them in making business decisions. Accounting technicians usually work in a support role within an accountancy firm or in the finance department of an organisation.

Depending on the route taken to qualify for the AAT and any experience gained, accounting technicians may undertake a range of roles, which will include:
- assisting with the preparation of accounts
- preparing the payroll
- dealing with invoices needing payment
- dealing with basic bookkeeping.

At a more senior level, they may be employed in audit work, both external and internal.

Working outside accounting

Wherever you work, financial knowledge is valuable. You could consider a career in financial advice, financial analysis or in insurance or investment, assessing people's needs and advising them on investments. A career in business management or consultancy would require you to have a clear understanding of how finances work and you could consider a graduate training scheme. Your skills would also be useful for jobs with HM Revenue & Customs.

Sources of information

Association of Accounting Technicians (AAT)
www.aat.org.uk

Association of Chartered Certified Accountants (ACCA)
www.acca.org.uk

Chartered Institute of Management Accountants (CIMA)
www.cimaglobal.com

Chartered Institute of Public Finance and Accountancy (CIPFA)
www.cipfa.org

CIPFA accountancy apprenticeships
www.cipfa.org/join/accountancy-apprenticeships/earn-and-learn

Institute of Chartered Accountants in England and Wales (ICAEW)
www.icaew.com

Institute of Chartered Accountants in Scotland (ICAS)
www.icas.com

'If you have accountancy qualifications, you can travel the world and work in many different types of business. It's a great training.'
Doreen aged 22, accountancy graduate, training as a chartered accountant

---

ANCIENT HISTORY

Are you fascinated by the ancient world as portrayed in films like Troy, Gladiator and 300? If you want to make sense of the world today, it's important to understand key events, individuals, movements and conflicts that have shaped history. A study of ancient history covers all aspects of the classical world from Ancient Greece to the fall of the Roman Empire (from about 3,000 BC to 500 AD).

The subject involves all aspects of classical civilisation, including social factors (women, slavery and religion), artistic and literary factors (literature, sculpture and architecture), intellectual developments (philosophy and education) and economic aspects of the societies. You will discover how these civilisations influenced the Western world and still do today. You will also understand Greek and Roman history in the context of their neighbouring civilisations and the interrelations of these civilisations. You look at how ancient historians as well as how modern historians interpret ancient history.

What do you study?

The topics listed give an idea of what could be covered. The exact content of specifications differs according to exam boards. You will need to check with your school or college about the exact options available to you.

The new specification is designed so that you can think critically, weigh evidence (literary and material sources from the ancient world), sift arguments, make informed decisions and develop perspective and judgement.

Both Roman and Greek history are studied through the interpretation and evaluation of original sources in translation

All your study periods will come from the period 3,000 BC to 500 AD.

You study topics in breadth and in depth.

A breadth or period study looks at a topic over a period of time so that you can understand the process of change, both long term and short term.

Depth studies focus on a substantial and coherent short time span so, you get to study the complexity of historical events and situations and the interplay of different factors within it. You would look at the social, economic, political, religious, technological and military factors.

Topics you may study include:

Greek breadth or period study
- Relations between Greek and non-Greek states, 492–404 BC
- The interrelations between Sparta, Athens and Persia from 492 to 404 BC

Greek depth study
- The Politics and Society of Sparta, 478–404 BC
- The Politics and Culture of Athens, c.460–399 BC
- The Rise of Macedon, 359–323 BC

Roman breadth or period study
- The Julio-Claudian Emperors, 31 BC–AD 68
- The reigns of Augustus, Tiberius, Gaius, Claudius and Nero

Roman depth study
- The Breakdown of the Late Republic, 88–31 BC
- The Flavians, AD 68–96
- Ruling Roman Britain, AD 43–128

All the texts are studied in English and you might get the opportunity to visit sites in the ancient world to put your studies in context.

There is a GCSE in ancient history and also one in classical civilisation, which will be a useful preparation for the subject, although not essential.

Latin or Greek can provide valuable background to the ancient history A level even though your texts are in English. A good English GCSE is required for this course.

Subject combinations
If you plan to take a degree in ancient history, an ancient history A level is useful preparation although not always required by universities. Some require history or classical civilisation A levels. Occasionally a GCSE in a modern language is required, but otherwise any subject that demands similar research and essay-writing techniques will be useful. This would include subjects such as history, English, and politics.

If you are taking ancient history with an archaeology degree in mind, a science subject at A level is often preferred; you would be expected to have it at GCSE level. For degrees in archaeological sciences, science A levels are required.

Higher education options

Degree-level study

Ancient history degrees involve a first year spent developing general background knowledge about the subject, plus the basic skills needed to analyse and interpret historical data. You are not expected to have learned an ancient language at school but most courses allow you to learn Latin, Greek or even Egyptian or Sumerian. In the second and third year, courses include a broader range of topics, but may also allow you to specialise in a specific area such as Greek, Roman, Egyptian or near eastern ancient history. You may be able to go on study trips to areas or countries relevant to your chosen options. Some courses offer the option of study abroad including one course that offers a year in China. There is a specialist degree in ancient Mediterranean civilisations.

Degree subject combinations

Many students at university combine ancient history with a related subject such as archaeology, classical studies, Egyptology, Greek or Latin.

Ancient history can be combined with other history specialisms such as medieval history, or history. Each has a unique approach to the study of past societies and provides you with a wider perspective on your studies of ancient civilisations. Subjects that look at political, cultural, religious and economic factors in human societies work especially well with ancient history. These include English, business studies, religious studies, philosophy, politics, anthropology, economics, history of art and modern languages.

Other higher education qualifications

There are no ancient history foundation degrees but there are related subjects such as history, heritage and archaeology, archaeology and historic landscape conservation – giving you a mixture of practical and theoretical work, and environmental conservation and heritage management.

Relevance to other subjects?

Ancient history has a number of related areas. Archaeology can be an ideal progression from ancient history A level. Medieval history and medieval studies focus on the origins and development of societies between about AD 400 and 1500. Celtic studies, Welsh, Irish and Scottish history cover the languages and cultures of the peoples who have lived in the British Isles since before the arrival of the Romans and Anglo-Saxons, although there are Anglo-Saxon courses as well. Classical civilisation courses are often similar to ancient history but have a specific focus on Greece and Rome, and include more literature, usually in translation.

Courses in classics, Latin and Greek cover similar ground, but the literary and historical sources are studied in the original so much more time is spent on language work.

Important advice

As A level ancient history is rarely a requirement for entry to an ancient history degree, choosing to study the subject demonstrates a genuine interest. This could play an important part in whether or not you are offered a place. Evidence of such interest can come from visiting sites of historic interest whenever you have the chance, getting involved in archaeological digs as a volunteer, volunteering at museums and heritage centres and reading as much as you can about the subject in your spare time.

Future careers

After A levels

As a student of A level ancient history, you will have gained skills in evaluating different types of evidence, placing them in context, and presenting them in a clear and balanced way. These are exactly the skills you need to work in areas such as management, sales and marketing. You might also want to consider jobs as a museum or library assistant. Look at apprenticeship opportunities in these areas.

After a degree

Working in ancient history

It is very unlikely that a degree in ancient history will lead to a career that will use your specialist knowledge to any great extent. For example, to teach the subject in schools you would need to be able to teach another subject as well, so you would need to consider a combined degree. Ancient history is clearly related to archaeology, but again there are specialist archaeology degrees, many of which involve an element of scientific analysis. To work as an archaeologist, therefore, you should aim either for a degree in archaeology or a combined degree in ancient history and archaeology. However, there could be opportunities in the heritage industry working in museums and other attractions.

Working outside ancient history

The skills of an ancient historian – research, analysis and reasoning – are attractive to employers in many professions. Graduates in ancient history go on to careers in a wide range of areas including business, education and the media. Your research skills could also prove valuable for a career in law, as an understanding of the systems of control used within classical civilisations (in particular, that of the Romans) is helpful in understanding the origins of our present-day legal system.

Sources of information

Council for British Archaeology
www.archaeologyuk.org

https://ccskills.org.uk/careers/advice/any/heritage/

www.besthistorysites.net

www.history.org.uk

'The best thing about my course is the choice available. You get to study so much more than the traditional Greece and Rome that most unis offer. You can study Egyptian and Sumerian cultures and you have the option to go to Greece or Rome as part of the course.' Susan, studying an ancient history BA

ARCHAEOLOGY

Archaeology is the study of past societies through their material remains and environmental context. This includes artefacts, buildings, burials and landscapes. Methods of data collection and analysis include excavation, survey and artefact studies, utilising a range of scientific and theoretical approaches. The new specification examines the impact of new techniques in archaeology such as remote sensing as well as looking at ethical issues such as the use of metal detectors.

What do you study?

The topics listed give an idea of what could be covered. The exact content of specifications differs according to exam boards. You will need to check with your school or college about the exact options available to you.

Archaeology in practice

You look at the techniques of modern archaeology and the dramatic impact of scientific techniques, particularly in reconnaissance, post-excavation and dating, and the impact of new discoveries on our understanding of human evolution. You look at archaeological evidence, archaeological sites and how landscapes can be discovered, explored and recorded without excavation using for example, remote sensing. You learn about the principles, processes and techniques used to record excavations, including the high-tech techniques used after an excavation by archaeologists to analyse and record the most common types of material recovered from the archaeological record. You also learn techniques for dating and interpreting artefacts and how archaeological remains are preserved and protected.

Debates in world archaeology

This looks at current debates in world archaeology and different theories and arguments for these topics. You might cover:

Political and ethical debates in world archaeology – ethics surrounding the use of metal detectors, funding, the social and economic value of archaeology, the concept of world heritage, the impact of war and political extremism on archaeological sites and collections, the relationship between local populations and western archaeologists, studying human remains or excavating sacred or burial sites.

Debates about human evolution and human interaction with the environment – the impact of scientific evidence based on our understanding of key changes in human development and evolution over the last three million years.

The development of modern human patterns of behaviour including pair-bonding, meat-eating, residential bases, tool use and hunting; the lineage of anatomically modern humans with particular reference to the role of Africa and the impact of recent discoveries in Asia. The changing place of humans in nature and human interaction with their environment over the long term including evidence for mass-extinctions. The impact of climate and environmental change upon human evolution.

Other factors impacting on human evolution including competition, natural selection and diet. How humans were able to adapt to ice age Europe. The changing evidence base for evolution and the importance of developments in dating, DNA, primate studies and recent fossil discoveries.

Themes in world archaeology: in-depth study

This develops your knowledge and understanding of the culture of two particular periods based on what archaeological evidence can tell us. You examine the economic basis and settlements of each culture and also look at:
  * social organisation and why this may have developed
  * the belief system(s) and rituals
  * art
  * technology.

The themes are:
  * the ice age settlement of central and western Europe
  * the Neolithic transformation of Europe.

Themes in world archaeology: breadth studies

You will also study two breadth studies. These focus on a different thematic area and you choose three different archaeological themes.

Examples are:
  * the cradle of humanity ? Lower Palaeolithic Africa
  * the spread of human species across the world
  * ice age hunting societies of Eastern Europe
  * the origins of agriculture in the fertile crescent
  * the emergence of civilisations in South and East Asia
  * palace civilisations of the Eastern Mediterranean

- the Iron Age in Northern Europe
- Roman Europe
- medieval Europe.

You then look at these themes and see how they relate to
- people and their activities in relation to economics and material culture or
- people and their activities in relation to society in the past or
- people and their activities in relation to religion and ritual.

The course encourages you to develop your capacity for critical thinking and to see the relationships between different aspects of archaeology.

The A level has 20% coursework which consists of an archaeological investigation of your choice based on personal research and fieldwork. This investigation normally focuses on your local environment, using local resources and using the archaeological methodology you have learned.

The new specification emphasises the skills that you need in archaeology; developing and demonstrating your knowledge and understanding of practical archaeological techniques. You must be able analyse, record and interpret archaeological data as well as understanding the nature and types of archaeological evidence and what examining such evidence can tell us about past human societies. There is an emphasis on responsible archaeology including cultural resource management, the role of UNESCO, the purpose and impact of protective legislation, debates about preservation versus excavation, the impact of the trade in antiquities and attitudes towards metal detecting. You also look at research and rescue archaeology, the funding of excavations and preservation of archaeological remains, and the social and economic role of museums.

Archaeology practice is assessed using a mixture of multiple choice questions, structured short questions and essay questions. The course includes field trips to archaeological sites.

Subject combinations
Archaeology combines well with many other subjects such as science, art, geography, history, sociology and religious studies. Sciences are especially useful if you intend to study archaeology at degree level and some universities require at least one A level in geography, environmental science, biology, history, chemistry, physics, mathematics, computer science or geology. Archaeological sciences degrees require one or two science subjects.

Higher education options

Degree-level study

There are a variety of courses on offer and most courses cover British and European archaeology - Stone Age, Bronze Age, Iron Age, Roman and medieval periods. If you want to do something more specialised – like Egyptology or classical archaeology for example – then the choices are more limited. Although most courses offer practical skills, there are some that specialise more in practical archaeology. Archaeological sciences concentrates on the application of science to archaeology. All courses offer some element of field work. Some courses offer a placement or study abroad year.

Degree subject combinations

Many subjects are available to combine with archaeology. The most common are anthropology, ancient history, geography, classics and modern languages.

Other higher education qualifications

There are some foundation degrees available, in archaeology, archaeology and historic landscape conservation and history, heritage and archaeology. There is also a crime scene and forensic science foundation degree which contains some elements of archaeological sciences.

Relevance to other subjects?

Archaeology connects with a range of other subjects. You could consider courses connected with the environment such as conservation or environmental science. You will have skills in research and data analysis which could be used in IT or business courses. There are also strong links with history and classical civilisation so these are also possibilities.

Important advice

See if you can visit an archaeological dig to see how it is done. Your local museum may know what is going on in your area. If you can get 'hands on 'experience of archaeology, then this will really help your application.

Future careers

After A levels

You will have excellent research and administration skills from your A level study which could prove useful in many jobs. There may be apprenticeships in museums, heritage or tourism where you can use your knowledge and skills. Look out for cultural and heritage apprenticeships in your area.

After a degree

Working in archaeology

Archaeologists are employed in all sorts of places, not just on digs. They find work in national agencies, local authorities, museums, universities, planning consultancies and private practice, undertaking a wide variety of activities from field practice to laboratory work, information management to education, specialist research to artefact curation and display.

Many students take a postgraduate course after their first degree to improve their job prospects. There are a variety of courses available including bioarchaeology, osteoarchaeology, Egyptology, experimental archaeology, forensic archaeology, heritage, human bioarchaeology, maritime archaeology and paleopathology.

Working outside archaeology

A degree in archaeology can help with a number of careers including lecturing, the Civil Service, lecturing, professional consultancy, media and the arts. Archaeology requires such a broad range of skills that its graduates are well equipped for many careers, and have developed the ability to enquire scientifically but also to see broad patterns of change. Many graduates find work in the heritage sector: museums, historical tourism and for organisations like English Heritage and the National Trust.

Sources of information

Current Archaeology
www.archaeology.co.uk has a directory of current digs in the UK, some of which will consider applications from those aged 16 upwards.

Council for British Archaeology
www.archaeologyuk.org

Creative Choices – heritage careers
www.ccskills.org.uk/careers

'Make sure you do some archaeology before you apply. This could be something local. Try your local library as they were very helpful.' Sally, in final year of an archaeology degree

ART AND DESIGN

Art and design features in every aspect of our daily lives from the cereal box we grab every morning and the clothes we wear, to the trainers we walk in – they've all been through a design process. You will learn traditional drawing and painting skills, new media techniques and also theoretical terms. You will be encouraged to look at a broad range of artists and to review your own work in relation to what you have studied. You will also learn to analyse your own work as a way of improving and developing it.

What do you study?

The topics listed give an idea of what could be covered. The exact content of specifications differs according to exam boards. You will need to check with your school or college about the exact options available to you.

The new specifications in art and design offer the opportunity to study a broad-based art, craft and design qualification or to follow a more specialised pathway in fine art, graphic communication, textile design, 3D design or photography. Students following the broad-based pathway will be able to pick one or two specialisms as part of their course.

➤ **Fine art** – drawing, painting, mixed-media, sculpture, ceramics, installation, printmaking, moving image (video, film, animation) and photography.

➤ **Graphic communication** – interactive media (including web, app and game design), advertising, packaging design, design for print, illustration, communication graphics, branding, multimedia, motion graphics, design for film and television.

➤ **Textile design** – fashion design, fashion textiles, costume design, digital textiles, printed and/or dyed fabrics and materials, domestic textiles, wallpaper, interior design, constructed textiles, art textiles and installed textiles.

➤ **Three-dimensional design** – ceramics, sculpture, exhibition design, design for theatre, television and film, interior design, product design, environmental design, architectural design, jewellery/body ornament and 3D digital design.

➤ **Photography** – portraiture, landscape photography, still life photography, documentary photography, photojournalism, fashion photography, experimental imagery, multimedia, photographic installation and moving image (video, film, animation).

On all these options, your practical work will be supported by critical and historical studies – looking at a range of artists both from the past and in the contemporary art world to encourage you to develop a greater understanding of the subject and help you look more critically at your own work.

You also study how and why art works as a form of communication, the forms and styles that such communication may take and issues relating to light, colour, form, perspective and movement.

Drawing

Drawing is an essential skill for studying art and design at A level and beyond. It forms a core element of the practice of artists, craftspeople and designers. It can take many forms; at its simplest and most direct it consists of marks of pencil or pen on paper, though it can employ any media and be applied in two and three dimensions or time-based media.

It is recommended, but not essential, to have studied GCSE art and design to take the A level.

The AS level consists of a portfolio of work and an externally set assignment.

For A level, assessment is by a personal investigation which involves a written assignment supported by practical work and an externally set assignment which involves answering set questions and supporting your answers through your creative work.

Subject combinations

If you want to move onto a practical art and design course at a higher level the usual route is an A level in art and design plus an Art Foundation course. For more academic higher education courses such as art history, you will need one or two more A levels. If you are considering architecture or landscape architecture, it would be useful although not essential to have maths or sciences to support your application. A level art and design may not be acceptable as an academic subject for entry to unrelated degree subjects, so you should always check with universities and colleges.

Higher education options

Art Foundation course

The normal route to a degree in art and design is through a one-year Art Foundation course. This can be taken at local colleges of art, many further education colleges and several universities. The purpose of the Art Foundation course is to give you the opportunity to explore a greater range of media than is usually possible in schools and to help and support you in preparing a portfolio of work to support your degree course applications. It is designed to be diagnostic – that is, enabling you to explore the breadth of your interests and abilities within art and design, helping you make decisions about your future direction within the subject. To get onto an Art Foundation course, you normally need to have at least one A level, preferably in art and design, or equivalent.

Portfolio

Your portfolio needs to be of a high standard, and your A level course is the best opportunity for building that up. Your portfolio should consist of:

- drawing: a range of work including drawing from direct observation; drawing as problem solving; and drawing to develop and present ideas
- idea/design development: showing how you develop your ideas and designs, including sketchbooks and worksheets that show your development, experimentation with media and work in progress
- formal elements: work which demonstrates your understanding of the key principles of line, tone, perspective, colour, composition, form and space
- self-initiated work: examples of creative work which you have done outside of formal study
- contextual understanding: work which demonstrates your interests and understanding of arts, design and media practice such as illustrated essays, artist or design research and evidence of exhibitions you may have visited
- show reels/story boards: including a credit sheet to clearly identify your contribution to your work.

Some universities or schools of art may ask you to submit an electronic portfolio, especially if you are unable to attend an interview.

Degree-level study

Art and design degree courses range from courses in which you continue to work in a medium that you have already used, but more intensively, to specialist areas of art and design.

Courses can be grouped into four broad areas: fine art; graphic, digital and lens-based media; fashion and textiles and 3D design. Under these umbrella titles each course offers particular specialisms covering such areas as jewellery design, design crafts, computer games art, illustration, digital design, design for art direction, interior design, product design, textiles, advertising and branding design and many others.

In some areas, such as furniture, jewellery, fashion or textiles, you will learn methods and use materials that are completely new to you. Alternatively, if your interest in art is on the critical and analytical side rather than the practical and creative, you could consider a degree in the history of art.

Degree subject combinations

You can combine art and design with a wide range of other subjects, although this is more common on university courses rather than art college courses.

Other higher education qualifications

Not to be confused with the one-year Art Foundation courses that prepare you for entry to higher education, foundation degrees are available in many specialist areas such as graphic design, illustration, 3D computer generated imagery (modelling & animation), illustration, animation and visual effects, art of games design, photography and digital arts, digital media, professional floristry and floral design, furniture and fine product, fashion and textile design skills, fashion design, pattern cutting and construction, design and fashion technology, garden and design, web design. They are a mixture of work-based experience and study.

HND and HNC courses are available in art and design (fine art),graphic and digital design, interactive media - games art and animation, jewellery and silversmithing, graphic design, photography, production design and art direction in the film and television industries, specialist make up, fashion and textiles and product design.

Relevance to other subjects?

As the art and design A level can include such a wide range of subjects, materials and techniques, you will find it a useful qualification for many other degree courses.

Degree-level study in photography, media or cultural studies, drama (including stage, costume and lighting design), advertising and architecture can benefit from the experience that you have gained through A level art and design.

Important advice

If you want to find out more about studying art and/or design at a higher level, contact your local school of art/art college and ask about attending a degree show, where you can see the sort of work that students produce. Degree shows are usually held in the summer term. Many schools of art run part-time classes (often on a Saturday) for A level students, and these are designed to help you build your portfolio.

Future careers

After A levels

There are some design-related apprenticeships available after A levels. They are in areas such as graphic design, digital design, web design and development, printing/digital publishing, photography and picture editing.

You could also consider apprenticeships in retail display or merchandising (which includes window dressing and designing point-of-sale materials), interior design and styling, model making and producing props for film or the stage. There are also apprenticeship opportunities in jewellery manufacturing, silversmithing and allied trades and fashion and textiles.

After a degree

Working in art and design

Many design graduates do find work related to their degree either in the UK or abroad. It is easier for design graduates, although it depends on the specialism. Graduates have to be prepared to freelance and build up their career gradually through networking and contacts, or move into a related design discipline. Many degrees courses include classes in self-employment including marketing and networking.

Fine art graduates who want to work as fine artists often have to supplement their earnings from art by teaching or other part- time work. Some graduates undertake postgraduate study to learn additional specialist skills or crafts.

➢   **Art therapists** help children or adults with disabilities, or those who have suffered emotional or physical harm, to overcome their problems through work on artistic projects. This type of work requires further training at masters level.

➢   **Conservation/restoration work** could involve working in anything from paintings to books or furniture. Further training may be needed for this.

> **Fashion and textile designers** are employed by fashion companies, or work for themselves, creating fabric and clothes designs for organisations ranging from high-street stores to international designer fashion houses.

> **Graphic designers** work in a variety of settings, designing logos for companies or events, through to digital or computer games design. They also work in publishing, creating the covers and page layouts of books, magazines and newspapers. Many work as freelancers.

> **Photographers** work in studios or on location. Some are employed by newspapers, industrial or architectural companies or by businesses compiling professional portfolios for models or actors. Many photographers are self-employed and are responsible for finding their own work, running their business and the creative photographic work itself. Digital imaging is an expanding area, using photographic materials as the basis for the computer-enhanced images that we see around us in advertising, online and in films.

> **Product/industrial designers** use their design skills in the creation of products from pens to chairs and cars. There are also specialist packaging designers.

> **Theatre, film and television designers** work creating lighting plans for the stage, costumes for period dramas on television, and complete film sets.

> **Teachers** need to undertake postgraduate training. There are some postgraduate art teaching courses for primary and more for secondary teaching.

Working outside art and design

The ability to communicate visually makes you a good candidate for a career in advertising, marketing and public relations. There may be opportunities within the film or television industries, although this is a very competitive field. Arts administration is another possibility   where you might be responsible for running galleries, theatre companies and other arts organisations.

Sources of information

Chartered Society of Designers
www.csd.org.uk

www.creativeskillset.org

www.ccskills.org.uk/careers

British Institute of Professional Photography
www.bipp.com

'One piece of advice I'd give to somebody thinking about an art and design degree would be to not just rely on work you have done for your A levels when putting together a portfolio. Experiment with different techniques, don't be afraid to do something you haven't tried before and create work outside of your course.'
Susannah, graphic design undergraduate

'Make sure you learn dark-room skills as this forms the basis of everything you do.'
Simon, studying A level photography with French and art and design

BIOLOGY

Biology is the study of the structure and behaviour of all forms of life – plant, animal and human. It covers a range of topics, from cell structure and microbiology, through human anatomy and health, to environmental problems, forensic science, ecology and biodiversity. You explore basic scientific principles and also look at how advances in science have raised other challenges for scientists, society and the economy as a whole – for example, gene technologies and carbon neutral fuel. The new specifications develop learners as critical and creative thinkers, able to solve problems in a variety of contexts. They also have a greater emphasis on maths than before.

What do you study?

The topics listed give an idea of what could be covered. The exact content of specifications differs according to exam boards. You will need to check with your school or college about the exact options available to you.

➢ **The variety of living organisms** – biodiversity, taxonomy (the classification of organisms into groups and types), populations and ecosystems (how groups of organisms relate to each other and their environment).

➢ **Development** – tissues and organs, cell structure, biological molecules.

➢ **Continuity of life** – DNA, genes and chromosomes, genetics, RNA, meiosis, mitosis, protein synthesis, inheritance, natural selection, evolution including environmental factors, mutations, the genome and gene technologies.

➢ **Energy transfers** – respiration (how energy is released from food), ATP (transports chemical energy within cells for metabolism), glycolysis, exercise and the body, photosynthesis, energy and ecosystems, nutrient cycles, nutrition and metabolism.

➢ **Response and control** – perception of the external environment (through sense organs), interpretation (nervous system, brain), response (muscle action, control of the heart and ventilation, hormone release) adaptation to change and homeostasis (how an organism regulates its internal environment).

➢ **Transport and exchange** – how nutrients and waste materials are moved around animals, including the roles of the heart, blood vessels, liver, kidneys and excretion, transport of water and nutrients in plants.

➢ **How science works** – how ideas, theories and research are used in the progress of science and how these ideas and decisions impact on individuals and society. How scientists can communicate with their audiences with appropriate scientific technology. The implications of new developments in science and how this will affect scientific careers.

Each specification involves learning the practical, experimental and research skills needed by scientists.

Maths

10% of the A level marks in the written exams will assess the use of maths skills as they relate to biology. The standard is Level 2 or above so equivalent to the standard of the higher tier GCSE maths.

Practicals

Students need to demonstrate confidence in practical techniques so your practical skills will be assessed.

For AS level, this will be by written exam. For A level, the practical assessments are divided into those that can be assessed in written exams and those that can only be directly assessed by carrying out experiments. A level grades are based only on marks from written exams. A separate endorsement of practical skills is taken with the A level. This is assessed by teachers and will be based on direct observation of students' competency in a range of skills that are not assessable in written exams. A minimum of 12 practical activities are assessed (not under exam conditions). There is a single pass grade which will be on the A level certificate.

There are also additional biology specifications available. These are advancing biology (OCR) and biology (Salters-Nuffield). These specifications are different as they use a context-based approach so more real life examples are used. You therefore learn through actual, practical experience rather than just theory.

A good grade in biology or a double subject science GCSE is usually required. You will need to work with data and understand the chemical processes within organisms, so good grades in GCSE mathematics and chemistry are also important.

Subject combinations

If you are aiming for a science-based degree then mathematics, chemistry or physics are the best combinations. Chemistry is required for some biology degrees. It is possible to study biology without traditional science subjects and it combines well with psychology, sociology and PE. If you are considering physiotherapy with your biology A level, then check the requirements as sometimes an additional science can help your application for this competitive subject.

Higher education options

There is a huge range of courses in biology and related subjects like biochemistry and bioscience. A level biology is required for many of these courses. It can also be a requirement for degrees in medicine, dentistry or veterinary science.

Degree-level study

Biology is a demanding scientific subject, so an analytical mind, competence in maths, laboratory skills and a good knowledge of chemistry and biology are all important.

A typical biology degree will cover a range of topics in the first and second years, such as cell and molecular biology, microbiology, physiology and adaptation, and genes and DNA. Many courses include the development of employability and professional skills.

You usually specialise in the third year or have the opportunity to study other specialist topics such as biomolecular science, ecological and marine sciences, conservation and management, biomolecular science, bioinformatics, human molecular genetics, plant biotechnology, molecular and developmental immunology, pollution: impacts and management, sustainability, cancer biology, freshwater ecology or fisheries ecology. Field trips will be an important part of the course, offering the opportunity to study at locations in the UK and sometimes abroad.

Whatever the degree title, the degree format is likely to be the same; a degree in marine biology, for example, will still cover the broad range of biology topics as well as the specialist study.

There are many specialist and applied biology degrees; for example, anatomical sciences, biomedical sciences, bioprocessing of new medicines, ecology, environmental biology, forensic biology, marine and freshwater biology, human biosciences, human embryology and developmental biology, molecular biology and genetics, genetics, microbiology, molecular biology, neuroscience, palaeobiology, parasitology, physiological science, plant science, sports and exercise science and zoology.

Many biology and biology-related degrees offer a year abroad or a professional placement as part of the course.

Degree subject combinations

Biology is available in combination with a wide range of subjects and popular combinations are biochemistry, chemistry, geography and psychology.

Other higher education qualifications

Foundation degrees are available in biological sciences and specialist areas such as animal science, bioscience, human biosciences, microbiology, marine biology and coastal zone management. There are also related courses in animal management, countryside management and conservation and veterinary nursing.

Biology HND and HNC courses emphasise the practical applications of biology for a career. Examples include applied biology, applied bioscience, biology for industrial applications, biological sciences for industry and forensic science. Some courses are more specialised, offering training for careers such as environmental conservation management and countryside management, horticulture, animal management and garden and landscape design.

Relevance to other subjects?

Biology A level is a good preparation for many related subjects at a higher level, and in many cases is required or preferred. Examples include medicine, veterinary science, dentistry, nursing, physiotherapy, microbiology, biochemistry, biotechnology, pharmacy and pharmacology.

Important advice

If you are considering a biology-based degree, you will need to check that you have chosen the right A level subject choices, as many courses ask for another science. If you are looking at a specialist degree in biology such as biomedical sciences, environmental or conservation biology, or forensic biology, make sure you research the content carefully to make sure it is right for you. If you are interested in a research career, then you may want to consider degrees that are accredited by the Royal Society of Biology.

Future careers

After A levels

An A level in biology will give you a wide range of skills. Employers will like the fact that you are numerate, a clear logical thinker and a good researcher so business and finance jobs are a possible choice.

Biology-related jobs could be as a laboratory technician or assistant, working anywhere from a school or a university to a commercial research laboratory. Another possibility would be a dental technician (bridges, crowns etc.), a dental surgery assistant or a pharmacy technician. The study of biology is a good preparation for work in the health service, and with care providers as well as jobs in food technology and food manufacturing. A knowledge of biology could also lead to jobs in sports and recreation and jobs such as personal trainer.

Higher/Degree Apprenticeships are available as a food science technologist, life sciences technologist, healthcare science technologist and process development technologist.

After a degree

Working in biology

➤ **Research** – This can be 'pure' (not carried out with a view to its immediate use) or 'applied'. Pure research is mostly based in universities and often starts with studying for a PhD (just over a quarter of biology graduates undertake further study of some kind including PhD, MSc or MRes courses). University research posts beyond PhD level are usually on short-term contracts and are competitive. Applied research is also carried out in universities, although much is done in the pharmaceutical, food, medical and agrochemical industries, where you would study aspects of biology related to the design and development of particular products. Further study could take you abroad.

➤ **Medicine** –It is possible for biology graduates to take a four-year graduate course to qualify in medicine. Entry is competitive and you may be required to have taken certain science A or AS levels, even though you are a graduate. You will have to sit a selection test.

➤ **Food science** – This is a growing industry and there are opportunities in food safety, food development, food technology, plant science, consumer science and product development in the food industry. There are also related jobs such as environmental health, dietician and nutritionist. Some of these careers will require further training.

➢ **Healthcare** – Careers in the healthcare sector include physiologist, epidemiologist, medical microbiologist, clinical biochemist, cytogeneticist, pharmacologist, toxicologist, haematologist, histopathologist, immunologist, virologist, gastroenterology technician, pathologist and biomedical scientist.

➢ **Sports** – Careers related to biology include physiologist, sports scientist, exercise scientist, physiotherapist, epidemiologist, pharmacologist, sports rehabilitation and sports therapist.

➢ **Teaching** – An option where you can use your enthusiasm for your subject is to teach others. This could be in a primary or secondary school, college, university or teaching adults. There is a shortage of science teachers so there are incentives for training.

➢ **Other work** – There are opportunities for work in the Civil Service, public health, medical and veterinary laboratory work, forensic science and the National Health Service (NHS). There is also environment-related work, including consultancy in the private or public sector, pollution monitoring, environmental impact assessment and conservation work.

Working outside biology

Biology graduates have skills employers value such as the ability to think logically and being numerate and IT literate. Possibilities include finance, management and the IT industry.

Sources of information

www.futuremorph.org

Biochemical Society
www.biochemistry.org

Royal Society of Biology
www.rsb.org.uk

Institute of Biomedical Science
www.ibms.org

'My degree course is 50% environmental and 50% human biology. I am pleased that I found a course that matched my interests. It also offers an optional work placement so I am researching where I can go for this.'
Dennis, aged 19, biological sciences undergraduate

BUSINESS

A level business helps you to understand business today, in the UK and globally. You will look at issues such as: How does a business calculate its profits? How do governments get economies out of recession? How do businesses encourage you to buy more than you need? Are zero hours contracts acceptable? What impact does the internet have on your life? What really motivates people?

The new specifications focus on problem-solving and decision-making skills. You will learn how to use a wide range of business tools and models and apply them to today's businesses. You will learn to apply numerical skills in a range of business contexts. You are encouraged to follow business developments and think critically about current business issues.

What do you study?

The topics listed give an idea of what could be covered. The exact content of specifications differs according to exam boards. You will need to check with your school or college about the exact options available to you.

➢ **What is business?** The nature and purpose of business, different types of businesses and how they operate in the real world.

➢ **Managers, leadership and decision making** – what do managers do? Different leadership styles, management decision-making, managing relationships with business stakeholders.

➢ **Decision-making** – the process of decision-making in different functions within a business such as marketing, operations, finance and HR. How different factors must be taken into account such as the use of new technology (social media and digital marketing), market conditions and competition, ethical and environmental considerations. You will look at how to increase competitiveness in business and how different functions relate to one another.

➢ **Analysing the strategic position of a business** – looking at mission statements, setting corporate objectives and strategy.

➢ **Analysing the internal state of a business** – analysing the external environment to assess opportunities and threats: political and legal change, economic and social change, technological change and competition.

➢ **Strategic direction** – choosing which markets to compete in and what products to offer, what is corporate social responsibility, how ethical and environmental issues impact on business strategy.

➢ **Strategic methods** – pursuing strategies, making business grow and introducing new innovations. Protecting innovation and intellectual property.

➢ **Working globally in international markets** – how global businesses work and operating businesses internationally.

The new specifications have an increased emphasis on quantitative skills and a minimum of 10% of the overall marks will be an assessment of these skills at AS and A level. This will include calculating and interpreting ratios, averages and fractions, percentages and percentage changes, cost, revenue, profit and break-even. You will be required to use and interpret quantitative and non-quantitative information in order to make decisions.

There is no coursework for this A level. Most of the assessment material is based on real business situations.

It is not essential to have studied the subject at GCSE in order to study A level business. GCSE maths is essential due to the increased amount of quantitative work in the new specifications and English is often essential. There will be visits to local, national and even international businesses and you may undertake some work shadowing.

Subject combinations

An A level in business is not essential for the study of the subject at degree level. A level maths is required for some degree courses, especially for management science. Some universities may not accept economics and business as two separate A levels. This is because they find the areas of study are too similar. Some universities specify a 'broad skill set 'so prefer a combination of different subjects. This could mean that if you are offering maths and science they will prefer a humanities subject as your third A level. You will need to research this before you apply, whatever course you are considering. Some degrees in business may specify certain subjects at A level. GCSE maths is nearly always specified for degree-level study and Core Maths may be required.

Apart from that, business can be combined with almost any other A level subject. Modern languages are a good combination as learning a language can give you a great insight into a culture and from there how business works in that country.

Higher education options

Degree-level study

You will find there are hundreds of degree courses in business and in related subjects, such as marketing and human resources. Many are very popular, attracting large numbers of applicants, although entry requirements vary widely.

The first degree to consider is a general business degree. This is likely to be multidisciplinary covering a broad range of subjects such as accounting, banking, finance, economics, management, marketing and entrepreneurship. You will also find more specialised degrees such as business administration.

Next there are degrees where you would specialise in one business function such as accountancy, marketing, digital marketing, business information technology, project management or human resources. Some of these specialist degrees can exempt you from professional exams in, for example, accountancy or marketing.

Another choice of degree would be one that focuses on one type of business or industry, such as retail, hospitality, tourism or music management. There are degrees in enterprise and entrepreneurship if you want to start your own business.

Some courses have an international slant with links to other countries such as the USA and Australia. You will also find courses in international business management with Chinese and international management in Japan and Korea as well as Latin American studies with business management.

Degree subject combinations

Business can be combined with almost anything, but one of the most popular subjects is a modern language as this gives you added value with employers. Important business languages are French, German, Mandarin/Cantonese, Spanish, Polish, Russian, Arabic, Portuguese, Japanese and Korean. On these courses, you are likely to spend part of your course gaining work experience with a business in another country. This might be anywhere in the world and will provide a valuable insight into the way business is conducted in that country.

Other subjects such as psychology, politics, sociology and law can complement business by adding to your understanding of the environment in which business must function, as well as the people it employs. You will also find business included in many engineering degrees, or may study engineering specifically from a management perspective. There is also the option of a degree in construction project management.

Other higher education qualifications

Foundation degrees are available in business and business management and in specialist management areas such as project management, equine entrepreneurship and business management, events management, business enterprise, hospitality management, accounting, agriculture with farm business, administration and business technology, business computing, beauty therapy and spa management, travel operations management, wine business management, music business and golf management.

HND and HNC business courses are extremely popular and course titles include business and finance, business and marketing, and business and human resources. Courses are modular and offer a wide choice of options according to the institution.

There are also specialist business HND courses available including hairdressing management, accounting, law, travel and tourism, public services, business computing with web design, and countryside management.

Relevance to other subjects?

Business A level provides a good starting point for a degree in accountancy, financial services or management. Even if you do not wish to go on to take a business-related course you will have a good understanding of the business world, which could well prove useful to you in the future, especially if you go on to study subjects such as economics, law, media or politics.

Important advice

It is important to look closely at the contents of each business course. You will find that some courses require a higher level of maths than others. Some courses are very competitive. To give yourself the edge over other applicants you should try to get as much relevant work experience as you can. This can range from a weekend retail job to working in an office during holidays. This experience can help you to make good contacts, which could be useful later on if you wanted work experience on your degree course.

Future careers

After A levels

A level business gives you an idea of the range of careers available in business and shows employers that you have some relevant knowledge and interest. You could consider jobs in administration, accounts or trainee management. There are Higher Apprenticeships available in many areas such as the retail sector and in banks, building societies, insurance, IT, law and finance companies. There are Degree Apprenticeships available in banking relationship management and public relations. As a trainee or apprentice, you will study towards professional qualifications or a degree.

After a degree

Working in business

Business graduates enter a wide range of jobs, depending on the emphasis of their degree.

➤ **Administration** – within a public or private organisation. This could include buying business IT and other equipment, creating a good working environment through facilities management, administering staff salaries, car fleets or business travel. In a small business you could well be doing all of this and more.

➤ **Advertising** – working on behalf of clients to develop advertising campaigns for products from toothpaste to banking services.

➤ **Entrepreneurship** – many universities provide support for start-up and pre-start-up businesses and this is increasingly becoming a real option for graduates. Many universities have enterprise and self-employment societies to offer advice and support before you graduate.

➤ **Financial services** – assessing the needs of individuals or companies in terms of investment, insurance, savings plans and pensions. You may be self-employed as a financial adviser or work for an organisation such as a bank, building society or investment company. You could also train to be an accountant. About 22% of business graduates enter finance careers.

➤ **Human resources** – recruiting and training staff.

➤ **Management** – this could be in general management in a particular sector such as retail, or hotel and catering.

> **Management consultancy** – consultants offer help and advice on management issues, in order to improve business performance.

> **Marketing** – identifying the potential market for a product or service and devising the most effective way of selling it.

> **Sales** – increasing sales of a product by managing a sales team, becoming a sales rep, managing call centre staff or devising sales strategies and plans for a company.

> **Teaching or lecturing** – in schools or colleges. With the increasing popularity of business A level and higher courses, there is an increasing demand for good teachers.

Higher level study

About 6% of business graduates enter higher level study in subjects like management and business, international business studies and marketing. Business graduates might also consider an MBA (Master of Business Administration) but this is usually taken after some years of working in business.

Working outside business

A business or management degree is useful in almost any area of work, as you will have knowledge of how organisations operate and expand. Areas such as health, education and charities all value people with business skills and experience.

Sources of information

www.startups.co.uk

http://appointments.thesundaytimes.co.uk/article/best100companies/

www.businesscasestudies.co.uk

'Studying business has really made me interested in finance and how it works. I've started to read the Financial Times now.' Rachael, A levels in business, German and politics

CHEMISTRY

The principles of chemistry underpin our understanding of the world around us and are relevant to all areas of science, from the chemical processes in living organisms to the formation of stars and planets billions of miles away. Chemistry encompasses the environment, with pollution control, recycling and the development of biodiesel. In industry you will find it in the development of new foodstuffs, synthetic materials and medicines. Above all, chemistry is about finding solutions to the problems that concern us and our surroundings.

What do you study?
The topics listed give an idea of what could be covered. The exact content of specifications differs according to exam boards. You will need to check with your school or college about the exact options available to you.

➤ **Physical chemistry** – what determines whether a possible chemical reaction actually takes place (energetics) and how quickly it happens (kinetics), the properties of gases, liquids and solids, and electrochemistry. Covers atomic structure and the periodic table, amount of substance, bonding, chemical equilibria, Le Chatelier's principle and Kc, oxidation, reduction and redox equations, thermodynamics, rate equations, equilibrium constant Kp for homogeneous systems, electrode potentials and electrochemical cells, acids and bases.

➤ **Organic chemistry** – the chemistry of carbon compounds, the variety and complexity that has allowed life to evolve (it is this connection with the chemistry of living organisms that gives this branch of chemistry its name). Covers alkanes (the main constituent of crude oil), halogenoalkanes, alkenes, alcohols, organic analysis, optical isomerism, aldehydes and ketones, carboxylic acids and derivatives, aromatic chemistry, amines, polymers, amino acids, proteins and DNA, organic synthesis, nuclear magnetic resonance spectroscopy, chromatography.

➤ **Inorganic chemistry** – the chemistry of all the other elements and the ways that their properties are related to their position in the periodic table.

➤ **Experimental methods** – skills of planning, implementing, analysis and evaluation, qualitative analysis.

Maths

20% of the A level marks in the written exams will assess the use of maths skills as they relate to chemistry. The standard is Level 2 or above so equivalent to the standard of the higher tier GCSE maths.

Practicals

Students need to demonstrate confidence in practical techniques so your practical skills will be assessed.

For AS level, this will be by written exam. For A level, the practical assessments are divided into those that can be assessed in written exams and those that can only be directly assessed by carrying out experiments. A level grades are based only on marks from written exams. A separate endorsement of practical skills is taken with the A level. This is assessed by teachers and will be based on direct observation of students' competency in a range of skills that are not assessable in written exams. A minimum of 12 practical activities are assessed (not under exam conditions). There is a single pass grade which will be on the A level certificate.

There are also additional chemistry specifications available, for example chemistry (Salters-Nuffield). These specifications are different as they use a context-based approach so real-life examples are used. You therefore learn through actual, practical experience rather than just theory.

A level chemistry builds on and develops what you learned at GCSE, so you should have chemistry or science and additional science at grade C or above (or grade 4 or better with the revised GCSEs) before starting the course. You will need to be confident in handling numbers, as chemistry uses many quantitative methods, so you should have GCSE mathematics at grade C or higher (or grade 4 or better with the revised GCSE).

Subject combinations

Chemistry is an essential subject for some degree courses such as chemistry, chemical engineering, biochemistry, medicine, dentistry, pharmacy, pharmacology and veterinary science where it will need to be combined with maths or other science subjects. Combined with biology, it is useful for biology-related courses.

Studying chemistry can provide valuable support for a wide range of other subjects including physics, geology, environmental science and geography. It is a well-respected academic subject, regarded well by universities, so there is no reason why you couldn't combine chemistry with subjects such as economics, business studies, languages or any other.

Higher education options

A good grade in A level chemistry is required to study chemistry at degree level. If you are not quite up to standard for entry to an undergraduate chemistry degree or have chosen the wrong A levels, there are foundation years available for some courses, which are designed to fill gaps in maths and chemistry and prepare you for entry onto the first year of a degree.

Degree-level study

As well as courses simply called chemistry, there are many other closely-related courses such as analytical chemistry, applied chemistry, biochemistry, biological chemistry and drug discovery, chemical physics, environmental chemistry, medicinal chemistry and nutritional biochemistry. You might wish to look at subjects that don't have chemistry in the title such as food bioscience, natural science, ocean science, pharmaceutical science or cosmetic science. There are also MSci courses in chemistry; they usually involve an extra year of study, either for research or to specialise in management.

Many courses offer an industrial year as part of the course which could be in the UK or abroad. You will find courses linked to universities as far afield as Australia, Japan, Europe and the USA, offering a period of study overseas. Try to find out as much as you possibly can about the courses that interest you, and make sure you understand exactly what you'll be letting yourself in for.

Degree subject combinations

If you do not want to specialise in chemistry alone, you can combine it with other science subjects such as astrophysics, nanotechnology, pharmacology or forensic science. There are also degree programmes combining chemistry with non-science subjects, for example, modern languages, IT, law and management. Languages will be important if you will be studying or working in a non-English speaking country as part of your course. However, English is generally accepted as the universal language for science.

Other higher education qualifications

Foundation degrees are available in analytical chemistry, applied chemistry, biomedical sciences, forensic science, human biosciences and pharmaceutical science. These are linked to degree courses if you wish to continue studying after the initial foundation degree. HNC and HND courses are available in applied chemistry, applied science (chemistry), chemical science for industry and chemical engineering. In institutions also offering degree courses, you can often transfer to the second or third year of the degree course after completing an HND.

Relevance to other subjects?

A related subject to investigate is chemical engineering. This looks at the development, design and operation of industrial chemical processes, such as the manufacture of synthetic fabrics, plastics and metal alloys. You would need to be taking maths and physics with your chemistry A level to get into this. Chemical engineering can also be combined with other subjects such as energy engineering. Pharmacy is another option and A levels should include chemistry and two others from biology, maths or physics.

Important advice

Chemistry is such a huge subject that no degree course can cover it all. If you aren't sure which type of chemistry you want to specialise in then take a straight chemistry course to get a good grounding in the subject. You can then specialise later on, either in the later stages of a degree or at masters level. This allows you to keep your options open. A number of companies are willing to sponsor students through degree courses in chemistry and chemical engineering. University chemistry departments will have details of these companies.

Future careers

After A levels

Chemistry A level is highly regarded by employers and the knowledge and skills you will have gained will help you in virtually any career. However, if you wish to work within professional chemistry you will need to obtain some extra qualifications first, or your options may be limited. There are Higher/Degree Apprenticeships available enabling you to obtain higher level qualifications while working.

Examples are life sciences and chemical sciences apprenticeships which are relevant for those training, for example, as a chemical science technologist, life sciences technologist or healthcare science technologist, and also apprenticeships in manufacturing such as in process development, the water industry and food science. Laboratory science apprenticeships are another possibility.

After a degree

Working in chemistry

Most chemistry graduates obtain work as professional chemists or in related areas. However, chemistry is a very large and highly developed subject, so you can only cover a small part of it in a degree course. This is why about 33% of chemistry graduates stay on after their degree to do research and/or further academic study for higher-level qualifications.

There are many career options for the professional chemist, including the following:

➢ **research and development** – chemists work to develop processes for making new products such as plastics, drugs, fuel, pesticides, fertilisers, dyes and foods

➢ **production** – chemists are involved in planning the manufacture of products and in monitoring quality

➢ **support** – some chemists are employed to support research and production activities by searching technical papers for information and in writing patent specifications. They may also be involved in the selling and marketing of chemical products and in advising customers

➢ **technical writing and journalism** – there are opportunities in writing technical articles for scientific publications and journals, editing science books or websites, or writing more popular scientific articles for newspapers and magazines

➢ **Civil Service and local government** – chemists employed by government bodies monitor and advise on the safety of foodstuffs, water and environmental pollution, and chemical safety

➢ **forensic science** – chemists are employed by forensic science laboratories examining evidence relating to crimes

➢ **teaching** – chemistry is a shortage subject and there are incentives to train.

Working outside chemistry

A degree in chemistry is useful in many jobs not directly related to chemistry because chemistry graduates are numerate, have problem-solving, investigative and analytical skills, and good IT and communication skills, which will all have been developed during degree-level study.

Business and finance is a popular area and approximately 12% of chemistry graduates go into this type of work. Chemistry graduates are also employed by local government, the Civil Service and in many areas of industry and business including marketing, sales and advertising, arts, design and sport, and social and welfare professions.

Sources of information

Royal Society of Chemistry
www.rsc.org

Futuremorph
www.futuremorph.org

www.geoset.info

www.whynotchemeng.com

> 'To survive into the next century we need to develop imaginative new sustainable technologies including new sources of energy, new efficient materials, recyclable devices and clever new molecular-based medical solutions. Legions of humanitarian contributions to society have come from the chemistry-based sciences from penicillin to sewage treatment, from shampoo to anaesthetics and from paints to liquid crystal displays. There can thus be little doubt that the chemical sciences promise to make similarly revolutionary and beneficial contributions to the way we shall live in the 21st century. If the future is in anyone's hands it is in the hands of the next generation of ingenious young chemists.'
> Professor Sir Harry Kroto, Nobel Laureate in chemistry

CLASSICAL CIVILISATION

The study of classical civilisations allows you to look at many aspects of the classical world which are significant in the development of the modern world. It is designed for students with an interest in classical studies, but who do not necessarily want to learn Latin or ancient/classical Greek. The period covered is Greek and Roman civilisation, from about 3000 BC to about AD 500. The new specifications cover a wide range of topics including architecture, archaeology, art, classical thought, ethics and values, history, political theory, religion and beliefs, literature and philosophy.

What do you study?

The topics listed give an idea of what could be covered. The exact content of specifications differs according to exam boards. You will need to check with your school or college about the exact options available to you.

The new specifications are designed to help you understand, interpret and analyse a range of evidence from appropriate classical sources in their social, historical and cultural context.   You learn to evaluate and use this evidence to form informed evidence-based judgements and responses to the material studied. You learn to present these judgements and relevant information in a clear, concise and logical manner.

Literature (in translation)

You will study each of the following types of literature and suggested authors include:

➤ **Epics**: Epics by Virgil, Lucan, Statius, Ovid, Silius Italicus and Ennius (Latin); Homer (Iliad and Odyssey) and the Apollonius of Rhodes (Greek)

➤ **Extended verse**: Lucretius, Virgil and Ovid (Latin) and Hesiod and Homeric Hymns (Greek)

➤ **Drama**: plays by Plautus, Terence, Seneca the Younger (Latin) and Aeschylus, Sophocles, Euripides, Aristophanes and Menander (Greek)

➤ **Shorter verse**: poems by Horace, Catullus, Ovid, Juvenal and Virgil (Latin); Sappho, Pindar, Callimachus, Theocritus, Simonides and Bacchylides (Greek)

➤ **Non-fiction prose**: Sallust, Caesar, Livy, Valerius Maximus, Suetonius, Tacitus (Latin); Herodotus, Plutarch, Arrian, Thucydides (Greek)

➤ **Novels and fables**: Petronius, Seneca the Younger (Latin); Aesop, Achilles Tatius (Greek)

➢ **Oratory and letters**: Cicero, Pliny the Younger (Latin); Lysisas, Isocrates, Hyperides (Greek).

➢ **Architecture** - types of architecture studied include temples, palaces, theatres and amphitheatres, residential buildings, baths, stadia or villas. Examples include the Parthenon in Athens, the Palace at Mycenae, the Athenian Agora, the Pnyx in Athens, the Pantheon in Rome, theatre at Epidaurus, the theatre of Dionysus in Athens, the amphitheatre at Pompeii, the baths of Caracalla in Rome and the Villa of the Mysteries at Pompeii.

➢ **Artefacts and artworks** - you will study a range of pottery, sculpture, mosaics, wall-paintings or other specific types of artefacts and artworks. Examples could be an individual piece belonging to that particular type, i.e. the vase depicting Achilles and Penthesileia by Exekias (British Museum), the statue of Laocoon and his Sons from Rome (Vatican Museums), the Alexander Mosaic from the House of the Faun in Pompeii (Museo Archeologico Nazionale, Naples), the gravestone of Dexileos from the Athenian Ceramicus, wall-paintings from the Ixion Room in the House of the Vettii, Pompeii, the Warrior Vase from Mycenae, the Prima Porta portrait statue of Augustus, the reliefs of the Ara Pacis, Rome.

Classical thought

This is the study of key thinkers of the period and their works on ethics, religion and belief, the nature and existence of god or gods and political theory and philosophy. You will use the original source material (in translation).

Examples include: Aristotle (ethics, political philosophy, metaphysics), Plato (epistemology, political philosophy, metaphysics), Epicurus (religion and belief), Cicero (political philosophy, religion and belief), Lucretius (religion and belief, metaphysics).

You will be encouraged to make comparisons between the classical world and the world of today. The exact subjects you study will be chosen by your school or college. You do not need any previous experience of studying the ancient world or its languages in order to study classical civilisation A level. Assessment is completely exam-based.

You do not need classical civilisation GCSE to study the subject at A level.

Most of the work is essay based, and you will need to do additional reading beyond the prescribed lists. You might visit relevant places such as Bath, the Ashmolean Museum in Oxford and the British Museum in London or go to see some classical plays. There may be the opportunity to go on a study trip to Greece or Rome.

Knowledge of ancient Greek and Latin is not required but some students become interested in these languages and some schools and colleges can sometimes offer the languages from scratch.

Subject combinations

Some classics degrees require an A level in Latin or ancient Greek, and others will accept a modern language as evidence of your language skills and learning ability.

Classical civilisation can be combined with most other A level subjects, particularly those where essay writing and textual analysis are involved. Examples of these are English, drama and theatre, history of art, media studies, politics, history, history of art, religious studies and philosophy as well as a study of the classical languages.

It is a useful A level for archaeology degrees (although may need to be combined with a science subject at A level for some courses). Art, politics, geography and history are also popular combinations.

Higher education options

Degree-level study

At degree level, you may have the option of starting a classical language if you have not done so already. Some degrees with the title classical civilisation or classical studies require you to spend some time on language work, while on others it is an option. Many of these degrees are open to students who have not taken classical civilisation or any classics subject at A level. For some courses, classical civilisation, ancient history or history are preferred.

However, an A level in a classical subject does demonstrate an interest in and commitment to the subject. In contrast, degrees called classics, Latin or ancient Greek all involve the study of one or both languages. You may be able to start one of the languages (although not usually both) from scratch at university.

Degrees in classical civilisation cover a broad range of topics (look also for classical studies or ancient world in course titles). They include the philosophy, art, literature, religion, history, drama, science and archaeology of ancient Greece and Rome.

The classical civilisation A level would be a good preparation for a degree in archaeology and there are some specialist courses in classical archaeology. Classical civilisation is often a preferred A level for ancient history degrees.

For information on degrees in classics, Latin and ancient Greek, see the entry for Greek (classical)/Latin.)

Degree subject combinations

Classical civilisation or classical studies form a part of many combined degree programmes, which may include related subjects such as anthropology, archaeology and classical languages. You will also find combinations with a wide range of related subjects that require similar techniques of research and analysis of evidence. Possibilities include modern history, English, religious studies, philosophy, politics and history of art.

Other higher education qualifications

There are no foundation degrees in classical civilisation, but related subjects available include history, heritage and archaeology, and archaeology. There are no HND or HNC courses in classical civilisation.

Relevance to other subjects?

A level classical civilisation is worth considering, even if you are not thinking of continuing it beyond A level. The ancient world has helped to shape the culture and civilisation of Europe, its languages, literature, history, art and political structures. Classical civilisation is a good introduction to that world, and so is a useful A level qualification for many humanities degrees. Subjects such as English, history, history of art, drama, religious studies, modern languages and philosophy all benefit from a knowledge and understanding of classical civilisations.

Important advice

Your chances of being accepted onto a higher education course in classical civilisation or a related subject will be improved if you can get some first-hand knowledge of the subject. You can get this by visiting museums and sites of historical importance, going on archaeological digs or excavations, reading related material in your spare time and generally being as active in your interest as you possibly can. Remember that you may have to pay something towards going on an archaeological dig.

Future careers

After A levels

An A level in classical civilisation would provide you with a respected qualification for a wide range of careers. Even if there are few jobs that could immediately make use of what you have learned, the skills developed while studying the subject will be useful to you. These skills would include the ability to do research, analyse what you have found, reach an understanding about the people and society that you are studying, and argue your point, both in writing and verbally. There are some related jobs in museums and heritage sites and possibly apprenticeships in these areas.

After a degree

Working in classical civilisation

It is unlikely that a degree in classical civilisation will lead to a career that will use your special knowledge to any great extent, unless you decide to become a teacher or lecturer. Classical civilisation is related to archaeology but remember that there are specialist archaeology degrees, many of which involve an element of scientific analysis, so to become an archaeologist you should aim for a degree in archaeology. There are opportunities in museum work, exhibition design, galleries, libraries, heritage management or archive work, but you will be in competition with graduates in ancient history or archaeology. Postgraduate study in a subject like museum, information or archive studies could be an option to make you more marketable.

Working outside classical civilisation

Don't let the limited opportunities for using classical knowledge put you off a degree in classical civilisation. The skills in critical thinking, persuasive writing and self-expression provided by a classical civilisation degree are transferable to a wide range of careers. There would be opportunities in research, administration, media, the Civil Service, law, accountancy, computing, and business.

Sources of information

Council for British Archaeology
www.archaeologyuk.org

www.classicspage.com

https://ccskills.org.uk/careers/advice/any/heritage/

'Knowledge of our classical heritage is invaluable to anyone trying to understand culture in the present day.'
Gemma, taking a degree in history with A levels in classical civilisation, politics and history.

COMPUTER SCIENCE

Computers are an essential feature of 21st century life, controlling daily activities such as transport, medicine, banking and retailing. The rate of change and development in computer science is rapid so the specifications aim to help you to develop the capacity for thinking creatively, innovatively, analytically, logically and critically. There is a strong emphasis on computer programming and the maths used to express computational laws and processes This A level has been designed to equip students with an in-depth understanding of the fundamental concepts of computer science and then to progress to further training and study.

What do you study?

The topics listed give an idea of what could be covered. The exact content of specifications differs according to exam boards. You will need to check with your school or college about the exact options available to you.

➢ **Computer systems** – computer organisation and architecture, hardware components, processors, machine code, input and output devices, software, operating systems, programming languages, logic gates, Boolean algebra.

➢ **Software and systems** – the software 'life-cycle', from identification of requirements and problem analysis, through design and implementation, testing and eventually obsolescence; hardware use and design. Software development and design.

➢ **Logic and problem solving** – be able to develop solutions to simple logic problems, be able to check solutions to simple logic problems. Following and writing algorithms.

➢ **Programming** – different types of programs available for different purposes. Designing solutions to particular problems, how procedural programs are structured, the types of data and data structures, the common facilities of procedural languages, how to write maintainable programs, and how to test and run solutions. Functional programming using languages such as Haskell, Standard ML, Scheme, Lisp or Python, F#, C#, Scala, Java 8 and Delphi XE versions onwards.

➢ **Data** – how data is structured, fundamentals of data representation including bytes, binary, different coding systems, encryption, digital sound representation, databases including relational databases, database design and SQL.

➢ **Communication and networking** – communication methods, networking, wireless networking, the internet, internet security.

> **Impact and implications** – the impact of computing on individuals, organisations, the economy and society, and legal and cultural issues.

> **Big data** – managing data sets so large or complex that traditional data processing applications are not appropriate.

> **Computing project** – this non-exam project comprises 20% of the overall marks. Students are free to choose their own problem or investigation.

Some examples could be a simulation for instance, of a business or scientific nature, or an investigation of a well-known problem such as the game of life; a solution to a data processing problem for an organisation, such as membership systems; a computer game; an application of artificial intelligence; a website with dynamic content, driven by a database back-end; an app for a mobile phone or tablet or an investigation into an area of computing, such as rendering a three-dimensional world on screen.

Maths GCSE is very important if you wish to study computer science at A level because the new specifications must contain a minimum of 10% maths content. Computer science GCSE could be useful and you would be expected to have some experience and interest in using computers. GCSE English is often a requirement for computer science degree courses.

Subject combinations

A level mathematics and sometimes further maths is a requirement for some computer science degrees, and physics is an essential preparation for some of the more hardware-focused courses, so you may want to consider these.

Even if you do not plan to go onto a computing degree, you will find that computer science is a valuable A level in combination with many others. It could be taken alongside A levels suitable for careers in medicine, law, business, politics or any type of science. The course will help you to develop the capacity for thinking creatively, innovatively, analytically, logically and critically so will be very useful for other degree areas.

Higher education options

Degree-level study

There is a huge variety of computer-related degree courses. You should never read too much into a course title without checking but, in general, courses called computer science are more likely to have a theoretical bias. Computer science is about understanding computer systems and networks at a deep level. You may find yourself looking into the formal and mathematical foundations of computing, as well as learning how to design and write complex programs in high-level and low-level languages. Courses called computer studies are more likely to focus on the applications of computing. Courses simply called computing can fall into either category. Course titles are evolving all the time as the industry develops, and you will find courses in computer science (digital media and games) and computer networking. You could look at software engineering, software development, intelligent computing, data science and courses in cyber security and forensic computing. There is also a degree in ethical hacking.

In addition, there are engineering-focused courses dealing with, for example, intelligent systems and robotics, cybertronics, computer systems engineering and network engineering. There are also specialised degrees in artificial intelligence. Applications of artificial intelligence range from 'smart' controllers for household devices to computers that can converse in English, play games, conduct intelligent web searches or act as the brain of a robot.

Many degrees are sandwich courses, in which you spend some time in industry, with placements abroad often available.

Degree subject combinations

Many students combine computing with business studies or management, either as separate subjects or on a course specially designed to bring the two together (as in degrees called business computing, or business information systems, for example). Mathematics is a most available combination, as are business studies, accounting, psychology, sciences and languages.

Other higher education qualifications

Example of foundation degrees available are computing, business computing, applied computing, computing and systems design, enterprise computing, web design and software development, computing (networking and forensics), interactive media development, 3D computer generated imagery, communication and computer networks, creative computing, They are also available in more technical areas such as computer aided engineering, network computing, network engineering security and systems administration and cyber security,

HND and HNC courses are available with different specialisations, for example computing and systems design, computing and systems development, interactive media – games art and animation, information technology practitioner, computer networks technology and web development.

Relevance to other subjects?

You will find your understanding of computing useful whatever you study, and in some subjects it will be extremely relevant. It is especially important for business courses and all science and engineering courses that involve computers for control, data collection and statistical analysis of results.

Important advice

Some prospectuses give quite detailed information on the computing facilities provided, but it is also a good idea to attend open days, to find out first-hand what is available. It is also useful to find out what happens to graduates from courses in which you are interested, so that you can see if this is the direction you want to take.

Future careers

After A levels

Having studied computer science at A level, you will be a valuable asset to any employer. You could consider Higher or Degree Apprenticeships in IT and your skills and knowledge will be useful in many business, financial and technical careers.

After a degree

Working in computing

Graduates in computer science have career opportunities anywhere that computers are used by businesses and the public-sector.

➢ **Account manager** – acts as the interface between ICT and the users or customer, advising on the best solutions for different types of application

➢ **Applications developer** – writes and modifies programs to enable a computer to carry out specific tasks, such as stock control or payroll, typically for technical, commercial and business users

> **Cyber security specialist** – ensures that a company's infrastructure and systems receive an appropriate level of protection from external and internal security threats

> **Database administrator** – responsible for the usage, accuracy, efficiency, security, maintenance and development of computerised databases

> **Game designer** – devises what a game consists of and how it plays, defining all the core elements and communicating this to the rest of the development team who create the art assets and computer code

> **Information technology consultant** – gives independent and objective advice on how best to use information technology to solve business problems. The work includes analysing problems, making recommendations and implementing new systems

> **Network engineer** – responsible for the management of a computer network. This will include software installation and configuration, upgrades, diagnostics and troubleshooting

> **Software engineer** – specifies, develops, documents and maintains computer software programs in order to meet client or employer needs

> **Software developer** – takes the specification for the requirements of a computer system and designs the system including hardware, software, communications, installation, testing and maintenance

> **Systems operator** – sets up the computer operating systems and standard software services essential to the operation of any computer

> **Teacher** – computing is a shortage subject and there may be bursaries available for training

> **Web developer** – responsible for programming the code that tells a website how to function. A developer builds a web site from the bottom up, which means designing the web site in such a way that both old and new end users have no difficulty navigating the site.

Working outside computing

Computing graduates working outside the computing industry or specialist IT departments can put their skills and knowledge to work in business, administration or finance. All businesses need a good knowledge and understanding of computers among their general management staff. Computing graduates will have mathematical modelling ability combined with problem-solving and project management skills, which will make them attractive to a much wider range of employers.

Sources of information

BCS, The Chartered Institute for IT
www.bcs.org

www.thetechpartnership.com/tech-future-careers/

> *'Working as a consultant means lots of variety. Through a project lifecycle, my day can vary between back-to-back workshops, writing specifications and testing the solution. On a typical day, however, I'll arrive at the client's site and support them with defining their requirements, capturing them and relaying the result to our offshore resources.'*
> Luke, graduate IT consultant

DANCE

Dance A level is designed to meet the needs of students who wish to study dance in depth. On this course you will gain experience of choreography and performance, and you will be encouraged to think critically about dance. You don't have to be a wonderful dancer but you do need to be motivated and fairly fit. You don't need any prior qualifications to take dance A level and your experience of dance need not have taken place at school.

What do you study?

The topics listed give an idea of what could be covered. The exact content of specifications differs according to exam boards. You will need to check with your school or college about the exact options available to you.

Core areas you will explore include dance technique, the art of choreography, anatomy, health and fitness, the history of dance and the analysis of specified professional works and performances.

50% of the A level assessment is performance-based and 50% is examined by a written exam. The specification requires students to 'develop, demonstrate and articulate practical and theoretical knowledge, understanding and experience of technical and performance skills, the process and art of choreography, the interrelationship between the creation, presentation and viewing/appreciation of dance works, the development of dance placed within an artistic and cultural context, professional dance works and the significance of these works and subject specific terminology and its use.'

➢ **Performance and choreography** – this part of the course assesses students on a solo performance linked to a specified practitioner within an area of study, a performance in a quartet and group choreography. You will learn how to create and perform pieces as well as performing from notated scores. You will gain the knowledge and skills required to choreograph for a group.

➢ **Safe practice** – this includes safeguarding your own health when dancing and knowledge of basic anatomy and physiology. It includes an awareness of correct alignment, technical accuracy, appropriate dancewear and presentation of self and a healthy approach to training, including lifestyle.

➢ **Critical engagement** – this will involve how to analyse, for example, how a dance is created and look at it critically to increase your enjoyment of what you see. You look at how professional dance works and study professional dancers.

You will examine set works and evaluate the performance and everything that has brought it into being, not just the choreography but also the costume, set design, dance company and the music.

Rooster (Christopher Bruce, 1991). Performance by the Rambert Dance Company (formerly Ballet Rambert). You will study the work of the Rambert Dance Company between 1966–2002 .This will involve an in-depth study of the company, their style and choreographic approach. You also study in-depth two works from particular artists within the company from: Glen Tetley, Robert North, Richard Alston, Siobhan Davies and Ashley Page.

Students can choose one further set work from the following works and styles:

- Giselle (Jean Coralli and Jules Perrot, 1841) – the romantic ballet period
- Appalachian Spring (Martha Graham, 1944) the origins of American modern dance 1900–1945
- Singin' in the Rain (Stanley Donen and Gene Kelly, 1952) - American jazz dance 1940–1975
- Sutra (Sidi Larbi Cherkaoui, 2008) – the independent contemporary dance scene in Britain 2000–present

This will involve a study of the genre and name artists as well as the actual work.

The written exam will include essay questions on the set work and the area of study.

GCSE dance at grade C (or grade 4 or better with the revised GCSE) is an advantage, but is not essential; however some formal experience in dance is required.

You will participate in practical dance and choreography classes. Theoretical study will involve watching professional works and discussing them. Notation lessons will involve both practical and theory work. You will take part in workshops including dance technique, choreography, anatomy, dance notation and dance analysis. Your course may include visits to local and national dance performances, and workshops with visiting dance companies.

Subject combinations

Drama and music are obvious choices, but you could consider media studies, English language, English literature, psychology, biology, and physical education. Some dance degrees prefer A levels offering writing skills, such as English or history, especially if there is an academic element to the course.

Further education options

Some further education colleges run dance foundation courses. The course content for these courses varies considerably but usually includes an emphasis on dance technique with some choreography and dance appreciation. They may include GCSEs, A levels or BTEC performing arts courses. It is also worth remembering that many vocational dance courses take students from the age of 16.

Higher education options

Degree-level study

If you want to become a professional dancer, the most common route is to train at a specialist dance school or college. Entrance requirements vary and competition for places is fierce. Most of the courses last three years and some lead to a degree, although they are mostly Diplomas. You do not necessarily need a degree to become a dancer so it is worth considering all your options.

Some colleges of higher education and universities run dance degrees. These vary in their content and course titles include dance, dance and professional practice and dance studies. Besides practical dance training, these courses have an academic content, covering areas such as the physiology of movement, dance analysis, dance history and the sociology of dance. Some are not intended as courses for professional performers but more of a general education for those who want to be dance teachers, company administrators, and education officers or to work in a related area. You will need to look at the content carefully to find out which course is suitable for you. You might want to consider a performing arts course or a specialist dance area, for example contemporary dance, dance theatre, modern ballet or dance: urban practice. Your choice will depend on how much further dance training or performing you want to do and whether you want to specialise in a particular area, for example musical theatre.

Degree subject combinations

Apart from the more obvious combinations such as music, drama, education or movement studies, there are some less obvious combinations such as biology, criminology and international studies.

Other higher education qualifications

Foundation degrees include dance, performing arts, musical theatre, teaching dance in the private sector and theatre arts (dance).

There are HNDs and HNCs in dance and performing arts. You may be able to transfer onto a performing degree after these courses.

Relevance to other subjects?

Depending on your A level choice you could consider degrees in music theatre and entertainment management, theatre studies, teaching, stage management ,technical theatre, live event management, PE, English literature, media studies, communication studies and music.

Important advice

Make sure you do your research into the right type of degree for you. How much performing do you want? Do you want to study other subjects? What facilities are there? It is important to make the right choice of degree in this area.

You might think it won't happen to you – but dancers are prone to injury. So if you are considering a career in dance or the performing arts it is always worth choosing some academic subjects at A level, just in case you ever need to retrain or if you need to work between dance jobs.

Future careers

After A levels

It will be difficult to get a dance-related job after A levels, but you will have knowledge of the performing arts, anatomy and physiology as well as study, research and team-working skills.

You could work in the health and fitness or leisure sector, either in administration or as a leisure centre assistant, or train to become a personal trainer. There are apprenticeships in leisure management and sports development .You might find work within the performing arts sector, such as front-of-house or box office work. There are apprenticeships in community arts, technical theatre and the music business.

After a degree

Working in dance

If you don't become a professional dancer, there is related work in the fields of choreography, dance therapy, dance teaching and arts administration. For many of these careers you will need to undertake further training, such as a PGCE in dance teaching and postgraduate courses for dance therapy and dance movement therapy.

There are postgraduate courses specialising in dance including performance, dance science, dance anthropology, dance cultures and choreography.

Working outside dance

If you have studied an academic dance degree, you will be able to compete with graduates for jobs where graduates are accepted with any degree subject. This could include anything from the Armed Forces to jobs in business, IT, finance and administration. You could consider jobs connected with the performing arts in some way, such as arts administration or marketing, theatre management or community arts work. As you will have a good understanding of health and fitness, you may wish to consider jobs in fitness centres, gyms, personal training or working in health promotion in jobs such as a healthy lifestyles officer. You might consider also working in an allied healthcare profession or complementary medicine by becoming a physiotherapist, osteopath, Alexander Technique teacher or reflexologist, although you would have to be prepared to undertake further training for all of these.

Sources of information

Council for Dance Education and Training
www.cdet.org.uk

Dance UK
www.danceuk.org

National Resource Centre for Dance
www.surrey.ac.uk/nrcd/

www.young-dancers.org

www.dancing-times.co.uk

> *'Remember that dancing is 95% mental so a positive mind set is a must.'*
> Hannah, dance graduate

DESIGN AND TECHNOLOGY (fashion and textiles)

The UK's fashion industry makes a huge contribution to the economy. It employs hundreds of thousands of people and is one of our most sought-after exports. This new A level aims to support this developing industry by giving students a solid understanding of the commercial, creative and technical sides of the trade. You will learn about influential and iconic designers, the history of the industry and its importance to society. You will also develop practical, technical, creative and business skills and gain a real understanding of what it means to be a designer. You will gain the knowledge and skills for further study or fashion industry apprenticeships.

What do you study?

The topics listed give an idea of what could be covered. The exact content of specifications differs according to exam boards. You will need to check with your school or college about the exact options available to you.

➤ **Materials and their applications** – the different types and qualities of materials and how they are used in design and manufacture. Investigating the qualities of materials e.g. flammability, crease resistance, shrink resistance. How products should be designed and manufactured efficiently, cost effectively and with care for environmental concerns. Efficient use of materials and manufacturing processes. Health and safety in the workplace.

➤ **Product development and improvement** – evaluating existing products and how they can be improved in terms of how they look and fit and meet design specifications. Inclusive design: looking at how designs are developed to be used by a wide range of clients such as children, disabled people and the elderly. Assessing the feasibility of products and designs by analysing different types of data.

➤ **Understanding customer needs** – looking at different data such as market research, ergonomic and anthropometric (the measurement of the size and proportions of the human body) needs.

➤ **Design illustration and communication** – learning design skills to produce good-quality designs; using business methods and skills to analyse market trends; developing communication skills for presentations.

➤ **Computer aided design** – how it is used to develop ideas and products and its industrial applications such as pattern construction and manufacturing.

➤ **Copyright and intellectual property** – how designs (including logos) are registered and protected.

➢ **Enterprise and marketing** – how the fashion business works; trends and cycles in fashion. How products are costed to make a profit.

➢ **Design methods and processes** – creating design specifications; modelling designs, testing for manufacture; evaluating the product.

➢ **Design theory** – historical movements and key design movements such as punk, art-deco, minimalism.

➢ **How technology and cultural changes affect fashion** – e.g. street culture, sport and leisure, the influence of celebrities.

➢ **Developments in technology and manufacture of materials** – development of new fabrics and technology for manufacture.

➢ **Product lifecycles** – recycling and upcycling.

➢ **Design processes used in developing your own products**. How this process works in the fashion industry.

➢ **Critical evaluation** – developing the skills to evaluate your own work and the work of others.

➢ **Project management** – planning for accuracy and efficiency, quality control, quality assurance, international quality standards.

Specialist knowledge

Knowledge of fabrics used in manufacture and their qualities; blending fabric; different ways of finishing fabrics e.g. Gore-Tex; different aspects of manufacture such as seams, fastenings, finishing, trims, dying , printing, embroidery, smart materials and e-textiles. Use of ICT in manufacture. Pattern drafting and grading.

Practical work

You will develop a design brief and then undertake a substantial design and make task and produce a final prototype. In both AS and A level this is 50% of the marks and you have to produce a written or digital design portfolio and photographic evidence of your final prototype.

Maths and science

The course includes elements of maths and science to reflect industry practice. This could be equations to calculate how much material is required for a particular design or learning about how different fabrics are produced and the special qualities they have.

Subject combinations

Art, design and media subjects are required for A level higher education fashion courses. For some courses you will need to provide a portfolio of work. Maths and sciences are useful for fashion technology courses but, sometimes, good GCSE grades in these subjects are acceptable.

Higher education options

Degree-level study

There are courses in fashion and fashion design and also more specialised courses such as fashion and costume for performance. You might also specialise in a particular aspect of fashion design such as bespoke tailoring, fashion bags or accessories. There are textile degrees which may specialise in embroidery, footwear, jewellery, knitwear or menswear.

There are also more business-focused courses such as creative direction for fashion, fashion business, fashion business and promotion, fashion buying and merchandising and fashion communication.

The technology side of the fashion industry offers great career opportunities so look at degrees in fashion technology. Some fashion courses offer a foundation year if you chose the wrong subjects at A level, or need extra support.

Many degrees include work placements, in the UK or world-wide.

Degree subject combinations

There are combined degrees such as fashion design and technology, sometimes with specialisms like sportswear or menswear. Also fashion and dress history.

Other higher education qualifications

There are a number of foundation degrees available including fashion and textiles, contemporary fashion, fashion and clothing, fashion design, pattern cutting and construction and design and fashion technology.

HND and HNC courses are available in digital fashion, fashion and textiles, technical skills for tailoring and costume and fashion.

Relevance to other subjects?

Design and technology (fashion and textiles) could be used for entry to related art and design courses, depending on their specialism. However you will also have developed good business and IT skills as well as a knowledge fashion and manufacturing industry so you could consider business, marketing , IT and retail degrees.

Important advice

If you are considering a higher level course in fashion, it is important to build up a portfolio. This should include any work that you have done outside of your coursework. Some students go for interview wearing clothes that they have designed and made.

Future careers

After A levels

There are Higher and Degree Apprenticeships in technical fashion, product development and sourcing and jewellery manufacturing and allied trades. You may also find apprenticeships in retail management, IT and business administration with a focus on the fashion industry.

If you wished to learn a particular skill there are Advanced Apprenticeships in pattern cutting, dressmaking, garment technology, sample machinist, footwear, leather goods, saddlery, tailoring and technical textiles.

After a degree

Working in fashion

➢   **Fashion design** – designers usually specialise in one sector of the market such as menswear or children's clothes. This is a competitive area.

➢   **Textile design** – working for large manufacturing company or design house. There could also be opportunities with architects, interior designers, fabric or clothing manufacturers and retailers.

➢   **Fashion media** – jobs also include art director, fashion journalism or PR. There are now creative directors/researchers who have an overview of brand strategy and the ability to create and realise an effective creative vision across multiple platforms with a team of creative practitioners.

➢   **Fashion forecasting** –forecasting new trends and fashions, working many seasons ahead.

➤ **Fashion merchandising** – ensuring shops have adequate supplies of the goods the customers want; working with buyers and store managers to obtain products, distribute them to stores and present them to customers. May plan new ranges by analysing and forecasting sales.

➤ **Fashion stylist** – working in areas like magazines, videos, films or with individuals, creating the right style and accentuating the positive attributes of the people they dress, or creating the right mood or atmosphere.

➤ **Fashion retail** – roles include buying and store management. Clothing wholesaling has grown rapidly in recent years; the work could involve sourcing garments from around the world and selling them on to UK retailers.

➤ **Fashion technology** – fashion or garment technologists translate a design into a workable production process using their knowledge of IT and materials. This is a shortage area with opportunities worldwide.

➤ **Self-employment** – about 25% of designers are self-employed. They may work in a niche market, for example footwear or sportswear. Many degree courses offer training in skills for self-employment.

Working outside fashion

With a creative flair and an eye for detail there are related areas of design such as exhibition design or web design. You might also consider event management or conference organisation. You will have developed an understanding of how business and technology works so you could consider careers in business, IT and management.

Sources of information

Creative Skillset
www.creativeskillset.org - fashion and textiles

Fashion forecasting
www.trendzoom.com

www.fashionunited.uk

> *'After graduating I had a choice of jobs. You have the choice of working in this country or abroad. It's nice to know that my degree is in demand.'*
> Pamela, fashion technology graduate

DESIGN AND TECHNOLOGY (product design)

Everything that has been made has been designed. You will learn what makes for good design solutions and how design affects society and the environment. Central to the subject is the design process, which will teach you how to tackle real-life problems in a practical way. You will get involved in the design and manufacture of your own products as well as learning about how this process operates in industry.

You must be able to communicate your ideas and will have the opportunity to use a wide range of graphic techniques, from traditional drawing methods to computer-aided design (CAD). You will learn to consider the materials and manufacture of a product in its design and will work with wood, metals, paper, card, plastics and some textiles, using your imagination and creativity to produce quality products. You will learn to evaluate your own work and the work of others.

What do you study?

The topics listed give an idea of what could be covered. The exact content of specifications differs according to exam boards. You will need to check with your school or college about the exact options available to you.

The new specifications have an emphasis on design needs and you develop an understanding of how current global issues, including integrating technology, impact on today's world. They also encourage your creativity, so that you will develop the confidence to innovate and produce creative design solutions as you develop your own designs and work with a client/end user. There is also a greater emphasis on maths and science.

➤ **Design and production** – You learn and develop skills in design and production, gaining an understanding of the properties and performance of a broad range of materials. You will look at processes and techniques of manufacture and how products are manufactured in the real world. You will consider broader issues such as the environmental sustainability of products and their manufacture, as well as health and safety issues, potential hazards and risk assessment.

➤ **Technology and production** – You will look at how CAD and computer-aided manufacture (CAM) and other digital technologies have influenced the production process. You also look at other factors in the development of products such as ergonomics and anthropometrics (the measurement of the size and proportions of the human body), inclusive design and consumer safety, including current legislation. An important consideration will be the lifecycle of products, their manufacture and maintenance, use and final disposal.

➤ **Design theory** – Design theory is an important part of the course and you will look at the influences and methods of historic movements and figures for example: Arts and Crafts – William Morris; Art Nouveau – Charles Rennie Mackintosh; Bauhaus Modernist – Marianne Brandt; Art Deco – Eileen Gray; Post Modernism – Philippe Starck; Streamlining – Raymond Lowey and Memphis – Ettore Sottsass.

➤ **Business** – There is a business element to the course which covers: marketing, market research and marketing analysis; innovation management; the use of feasibility studies on the practicability of proposed solutions; modelling the costing of projects to achieve an optimum outcome; budgeting and financial forecasting; planning for production – allocation of: employees, materials; deciding on the scale of production; selection of appropriate tools, machines and manufacturing processes.

You will also look at the importance of intellectual property rights to the designer, inventor and company, including patents, copyrights, design rights and trademarks.

➤ **Independent design and make project** – you will write a specification of your own project, plan, investigate and research it and produce your own product. This will be backed up by a portfolio of work showing how you worked on each part of the design process.

➤ **Maths and science** – 15% of the A level marks in the written exams will assess the use of maths skills as they relate to product design. The standard is Level 2 or above so equivalent to the standard of the higher tier GCSE maths. Science skills, knowledge and understanding are also an important part of the A level in order to underpin the theory and practice of design and technology.

Subject combinations

Design and technology (product design) combines well with other subjects. If you are interested in engineering, it would be a good idea to consider A levels in maths and physics. Design technology could also be combined with a BTEC National in engineering, although you would have to check that there is no major overlap with your school or college's specification for these subjects.

Higher education options

Degree-level study

Popular courses include product design, creative product design, product design technology, industrial product design, design products, sustainable product design and 3D design. Courses have strong links with industry and many include sandwich placements. Some courses get students to partner with commercial companies to work on a specific brief. Product design degrees usually include related subjects such as management, business and innovation. The design-focused courses will ask for a portfolio of practical work as part of the application process.

Product design degrees have different focuses and specialisms. Examples include: product and furniture design, automotive and transport design, product design engineering and sports product design. In addition you might consider degrees in architecture or architectural design technology, although you would need to check with institutions for their exact entry requirements. There are also some related degrees such as special effects and model making. Many degrees offer an industrial placement as part of the degree.

Degree subject combinations

Product design tends to be offered in combination with subjects such as business and management.

Other higher education qualifications

Foundation degrees are available in product design and 3D design. There are also more engineering-focused courses such as electrical or electronic manufacturing engineering and engineering design and manufacture. There are HNDs and HNCs available in practical product and spatial design and contemporary design and production.

Relevance to other subjects?

Combined with relevant subjects, design and technology (product design) can lead to engineering, architecture, design and art courses.

Important advice

You will find a wide range of product-design related degree courses available so you will need to spend some time investigating them. You will be developing a portfolio as part of your course, but don't forget that any work you do outside your coursework may be a useful addition to your portfolio when you apply.

Future careers

After A levels

There are Higher/Degree Apprenticeships in engineering, construction and manufacturing which could lead to technician-level jobs. Further training will be necessary for all jobs at this level and some apprenticeships lead to degree-level study.

After a degree

Working in product design

Product designers work in many business areas including consumer electronics, sports equipment, medical products and the automotive industry. Many product designers work directly for large and small businesses while others work for independent consultancies both in the UK and abroad. The skills learned in a product design degree make many other careers a possibility, and of course you could start your own business. Teaching is another option, as design and technology is a shortage area. You would need to undertake further training to gain QTS (Qualified Teacher Status) for this and there may be financial incentives to study.

Working outside product design

Good problem-solving, creative and analytical skills can lead into many other careers such as management, business and finance or a related branch of design and engineering.

Sources of information

Chartered Institute of Architectural Technologists
www.ciat.org.uk

www.ccskills.org.uk/careers

Design Council
www.designcouncil.org.uk

Institution of Engineering Designers
www.ied.org.uk

> *'You need the ability to use both sides of your brain – creative and logical.'*
> Gerard, industrial designer

DRAMA AND THEATRE

If you enjoy learning about all aspects of drama and theatre then this course will suit you. It is largely a practical course but also includes study of the work of influential playwrights, directors and theatre companies that make theatre so exciting and diverse. It provides the necessary skills to analyse and appreciate any play text or performance. You also gain knowledge and experience of all aspects of drama and theatre including directing, set design, and sound and lighting design.

What do you study?

The topics listed give an idea of what could be covered. The exact content of specifications differs according to exam boards. You will need to check with your school or college about the exact options available to you.

The new specifications encourage students to experience and develop skills in all aspects of the subject:

➢ **Actor** – developing acting skills – interpretation of character, exploration of style, voice, physicality and stage relationships with others.

➢ **Director** – developing interpretative skills when working with plays. Instigating ideas for performance and developing a directorial 'vision' when working on original material or texts.

➢ **Designer** – learning design skills and considering how design impacts upon an audience. Developing ideas for set creation, costume, props, lighting and sound design.

The specifications include:

➢ **live performance** – you will see live theatre performances, which will give you a means of comparison between theatre styles, playwrights, companies and periods. You will also create original drama presentations in which your group is entirely responsible for all aspects – developing an original idea, producing, designing and performing it.

➢ **theatre texts** – (as pieces meant for performance) how they are translated into a stage performance; how creative opportunities are presented by this process; how effectively they communicate the feelings and ideas that they contain. The performance texts studied for the exam will require students to articulate how they would perform in certain roles, design for certain scenes and interpret a text for performance, putting practical work at the heart of the specification.

Examples of texts include contemporary plays such as:

Accidental Death of an Anarchist, Dario Fo, Colder Than Here, Laura Wade, Equus, Peter Shaffer, Fences, August Wilson, Machinal, Sophie Treadwell, That Face, Polly Stenham.

Also 'classic' texts such as Antigone, Sophocles, Doctor Faustus, Christopher Marlowe, Hedda Gabler, Henrik Ibsen, Lysistrata, Aristophanes, The Maids, Jean Genet,The School for Scandal, Richard Brinsley Sheridan, The Tempest, William Shakespeare, Waiting for Godot, Samuel Beckett and Woyzeck, Georg Büchner.

➢ **set and costume design** – how these may be used to communicate ideas and add to the overall effectiveness of the performance.

➢ **stage lighting and sound** – lighting and sound management skills and their importance in the creation of mood and atmosphere, use of special effects.

➢ **masks and puppets** – the skills behind their use in theatre directing.

➢ **theatre practitioners** – includes directors, designers and theatre companies; theatre companies such as Complicité, Punchdrunk and Kneehigh and practitioners such as Antonin Artaud, Bertolt Brecht, Joan Littlewood, Steven Berkoff and Constantin Stanislavsk.

You may be able to specialise in a particular aspect of the subject such as performing, lighting, sound, set, costume, puppets or directing.

Drama and theatre is assessed by practical work (60%) and by written exams (40%). The practical work consists of being assessed on live performances and devising performance pieces using set texts. If you have specialised in an area of theatre such as set design, directing, or sound and lighting design this will be assessed in the practical exam.

Students may also be asked to keep a log of how they approached the practical work and how it developed throughout the whole process.

The written exams assess knowledge and understanding of how drama and theatre is developed and performed, and ability to analyse and evaluate the live theatre work of others. There are also questions around the set texts and around live performances that students have seen.

It is not essential to have studied the subject at GCSE in order to take the A level but you do need good grades in English. A genuine interest in all aspects of drama – performance, directing, studying plays and design, is essential.

Subject combinations

English and drama and theatre is a popular combination. Some theatre studies courses at a higher level require A level in English in addition to, or instead of, a performance-based one. You mustn't make the mistake of assuming that the work you do on set texts in A level drama and theatre is exactly the same as that done on set texts in English or modern languages. In the drama and theatre A level, you study the texts as a starting point and foundation for producing a performance rather than as literature. Drama and theatre is a subject in its own right, and not a variant of English literature. Other popular combinations are sociology, history, media studies, psychology and religious studies.

Higher education options

An A level in drama and theatre is not essential to study the subject at degree level.

Degree-level study

Theatre and drama-related degree courses come in many forms with different titles. Your choice of course will depend on your areas of interest. For example, how much practical work do you want in comparison to theory? Do you want technical training in lighting, sound, stage management, costume or set design?

Drama or theatre arts degrees tend to provide the most general grounding in all aspects of theatre skills and theory. You have the opportunity to choose options in later years in areas such as playwriting, design and physical theatre.

You might want to specialise and choose a course focusing on a particular aspect of theatre, for example lighting design, costume, technical theatre, theatre production, stage management or stage combat.

Many 'traditional' drama schools offer BA courses as well as Diplomas so you must research your choice of course carefully. Auditions will be an essential part of the selection process, especially for the drama schools. You have to be persistent and it may be worth reapplying if you are turned down the first time. You may be accepted later on, so waiting and getting more experience may pay dividends.

Degree subject combinations

You can combine a theatre or drama course with related subjects such as English, music, media studies and modern languages. Some courses offer flexibility in your studies. For example, you could study a module in new theatre writing, followed by performance practice, followed by directing, while being assessed on each as you go.

Other higher education qualifications

There are many foundation degrees in drama and theatre related subjects. These can lead to degree-level study or employment. Examples include acting performance, contemporary circus and physical performance, costume design and realisation, dance theatre performance, design in media make up, performing arts management, prosthetic make-up effects, media make-up, special effects make-up and hair design, stage management and technical theatre, theatre arts (prop making and special effects) and theatre media performance.

Examples of HNDs and HNCs available include performing arts, technical theatre and stage management, musical theatre and special effects make-up.

Relevance to other subjects?

Theatre is a form of communication and expression that looks at humans and how they behave in different situations. You will find a broad range of related subjects for which drama and theatre A level will provide a good background. These include psychology, history, sociology, politics and classical civilisation. Your ability to analyse and extract information from the written word would be a valuable skill in the study of any subject that requires work on texts, such as English, modern languages, cultural studies, media studies and philosophy.

Important advice

Courses involving practical performance or direction work will require an audition, where you may have to act, sing, direct or dance. In addition you will be judged according to how much performance experience you have and how much live theatre you have seen. You should try to gain as much practical experience as possible, by taking part in productions at school or college and joining local drama groups. For courses that involve a large design or technical element, you may be required to show evidence of your practical experience. This can be in the form of photographs or drawings of productions for which you have designed sets, lighting, costumes, etc.

Future careers

After A levels

An A level in drama and theatre will not automatically get you a career in the theatre but then neither will a degree course, although the degree route into the profession is more common. Acting is a competitive and crowded profession. It is virtually impossible to perform without an Equity membership card (Equity being the union responsible for professional actors and performers), yet it is difficult to get an Equity card without having been offered professional work as a performer.

You can get round this in two ways. Firstly by gaining further training at one of the accredited drama schools and thereby getting a student Equity card. Secondly, by earning in excess of £500 from the industry in an area of work covered by Equity.

If you are interested in technical theatre or the business admin side of theatre work, there may be some apprenticeships available with A levels or equivalent.

You could gain relevant experience and training in drama-related careers by working in a theatre as a box-office assistant or usher, or volunteer working on community, youth or amateur theatre projects.

After a degree

Working in drama and theatre

The professional theatre is full of people looking for their next employment opportunity, and it can be difficult to get work. If you have determination and a realistic understanding of the difficulties involved, it is possible to break into the industry.

➤ **Actor** – usually self-employed but may have an agent to search out and negotiate contracts. Actors move between the various media – theatre, film, television and radio – and can often make the most money by doing commercials, voiceovers and training films.

➤ **Costume designer or costume and wardrobe** – this involves the design and creation or hiring and buying of costumes for a play, and keeping tabs on a theatre's stock of costumes.

➤ **Designer** – some work on sets, others on sets and costumes and even lighting designs. Most have further training in the design field and are freelance.

➤ **Director** – responsible for choosing the actors; with the designer and lighting designer, working out the look of the piece. In rehearsals, the director works on the overall shape of the scenes, as well as perfecting the actors' performances.

➤ **Drama therapist** – a career where you use drama to help the recovery of people with emotional or mental health issues. Specialist training is required in addition to your drama qualification.

➤ **Education officer** – employed by many theatres to work with schools and colleges and arrange educational trips to the theatre.

➤ **Marketing manager** – finds a way to get 'bums on seats'. May work with a press manager to deal with publicity.

➤ **Sound or lighting technician** – often employed by a theatre on a full-time basis. Works with visiting designers and directors on the aural and visual environment of a play.

➤ **Stage manager** – responsible for running the production in rehearsal and performance. Tasks range from photocopying the script to managing the stage crew, and telling actors and lighting technicians when they are to 'go on' or 'switch on'.

Working outside drama and theatre

Any career that demands confident verbal and physical communication skills is one that a graduate of a performance-based degree would enjoy. A good example is sales and marketing. Your skills could also be used in human resources work, conference organising (including lighting, sound and direction), museum and other exhibition work, and advertising, where an awareness of the importance of visual image and design in the communication of an idea is vital.

Sources of information

Equity
www.equity.org.uk

Get into theatre
www.getintotheatre.org

Drama UK (which has a list of drama schools)
www.dramauk.co.uk

National Youth Theatre
www.nyt.org.uk

> *'Drama and theatre A level has given me confidence and I feel better able to communicate and express myself.'*
> Suki, taking A levels in drama and theatre, English literature and business

ECONOMICS

Economics affects everything around us, from the price we pay for a loaf of bread to the likelihood of people we know being in work. Economists are interested in all aspects of life, not only in the more obvious issues such as consumer spending, inflation, house prices, unemployment, wages and international trade but also in environmental pollution, how firms compete, living standards, how we behave as consumers, taxation, poverty, health, education and much more. All aspects of economic theory are applied to the real world – to what determines growth, unemployment, inflation, the balance of payments, the gap between wealth and poverty, and society.

What do you study?

The topics listed give an idea of what could be covered. The exact content of specifications differs according to exam boards. You will need to check with your school or college about the exact options available to you.

➤ **Macroeconomics** deals with the economy as a whole and looks at large-scale issues. You learn different theories of how the economy as a whole operates, looking at the standard measures of a country's economic performance such as inflation and unemployment levels and the difficult, and sometimes conflicting, measures governments can take to move to a more 'desirable' outcome.

➤ **Microeconomics** analyses the market behaviour of individual consumers and firms in an attempt to understand the decision-making process of firms and households. You look at wages, and whether markets are operating efficiently or not. You consider what happens if the outcome determined by the market is not desirable, for example high levels of smoking, alcohol consumption and obesity, and the actions governments can take to correct this market failure. Market theory is applied to the labour market and the theory of how wages are determined.

➤ **Global economics** looks beyond the UK economy and examines the theory behind (and the reality of) international trade. You consider the arguments for and against free trade and the benefits and drawbacks of globalisation. Theories of economic development are examined to explain why some developing economies advance whilst others do not, and what may hinder, or help, that development.

The new specifications are designed to encourage students to think like economists and develop the appropriate range of analytical, questioning and reasoning skills to achieve this objective. The subject demands that students develop a strong grounding in both microeconomics and macroeconomics, drawing on local, national and global contexts. There is a bigger focus on maths; 20% of the final A level mark is concerned with quantitative methods e.g. cost calculations, revenue and profit etc. Coursework is not included in the new specifications.

You must take an interest in current affairs, read a quality newspaper and get involved in discussion and argument. You will be required to carry out research on your own, and need to be able to evaluate the merits of alternative arguments. The study of economics will broaden your understanding of the business world and encourage you to evaluate the consequences of business and government decisions. It's a useful subject for anyone wanting to go into business and finance since it is included as a core subject in the examinations of all the professional bodies including law, banking, marketing and accountancy.

It is not essential to have studied economics at GCSE in order to take the A level. You need to have a good understanding of maths for the new specifications, so GCSE maths at grade A*-C (or grade 4 or better with the revised GCSE) is usually essential, as is English.

Subject combinations

Economics combines well with a wide variety of other A level subjects and popular subjects are maths, English, history, geography, philosophy, politics and modern languages. If you have chosen business studies as one of your A levels it may overlap with economics, and some higher education institutions may not accept business studies and economics counting as two separate subjects for entry. If you want to study economics at degree level, think about combining it with A level mathematics as this is requested or preferred by some universities. Some like you to have further maths A level but it is important to check this. Maths could really help your application as economics is such a popular course, and will also help you while on your degree course.

Higher education options

No previous study of economics is required for many university courses. If your school or college does not offer economics at A level, then business A level is considered as an alternative by some universities but it is vital to check with each institution.

Degree-level study

Economics courses typically begin with a broad-based first year when you study economics along with other social sciences. In this first year mathematics and/or statistics are often compulsory subjects, especially for students who have not done them at A level. IT and languages may also be available at this stage. In the later years of the course, you can specialise through your choice of options, which could include forecasting and planning, public finance or monetary theory, although some topics such as econometrics (mathematical economics), international economics, and labour economics are sometimes compulsory. You may also get the opportunity to study abroad or undertake a work placement.

Some universities specialise in different aspects of economics, so you should examine course descriptions very carefully to decide exactly which areas you would like to study. There are economics degrees available both as a Bachelor of Arts (BA) or a Bachelor of Science (BSc). BSc courses are focused more towards maths and quantitative methods.

Related course titles to look out for include financial economics, applied economics, international economics and business economics.

Degree subject combinations

You may choose to combine economics with a related area and there are combinations available in finance, econometrics (statistical methods used by economists), economic history, international business, management, banking and statistics. However, there is also a whole range of other subjects available such as politics, accounting, geography, international development, sociology and modern languages.

Other higher education qualifications

There are no pure economics foundation degrees but there are a few using applied knowledge; these include business enterprise and business management.

Economics features in HND and HNC courses such as business studies, accounting and marketing and some have options in economic development.

Relevance to other subjects?

Many students decide on a degree course in a related subject area such as business studies, finance, marketing, management science and international relations. In all these courses the study of economics is included, so your A level in economics would be helpful. The development of your analytical skills makes economics a good A level for law degrees.

Important advice

Some degrees in economics and business studies are run as sandwich courses, where part of the course is spent on a work placement. When you apply for these courses you may be considered on your suitability for employment as well as your academic ability. Try to get some work experience in a related area such as banking, finance or accountancy before you apply.

Future careers

After A levels

An economics A level is useful for many jobs after A levels. You will possess transferable skills in research, analysis and evaluation of written and numerical economic data, communication and working with others. There are Higher Apprenticeships in accounting, banking, business, insurance, tax, management consulting and retail management.

After a degree

Working in economics

The majority of graduates get employment in banking and finance, business management or computing. A numerate degree with problem-solving skills is very marketable to employers.

If you are considering working in economics you will need to consider postgraduate study. Just over 13% of economics graduates enter postgraduate study, and for graduates with non-economics degrees there are postgraduate conversion courses in economics although they do require some knowledge of maths and quantitative methods.

However, there are many types of work in which you can use and apply your economics degree.

➢ **Government Economic Service** – advising government departments on economic policy.

➢ **Economic analysis and advice** – relating to share, currency or bond markets or the profiling of industries or different economies. The most prominent jobs are in the City, but more economists work for large companies, advising on their products and markets.

➢ **International work** – for example, for multinational companies or institutions such as the International Monetary Fund.

➢ **Economics or financial journalism**.

➢ **Teaching or lecturing** – in school and colleges. You would need to undertake further training to gain QTS (Qualified Teacher Status) for this and there may be financial incentives to study.

Working outside economics

Knowledge of the economy and the logical, numerical and analytical skills that you gain through studying economics are valuable for many careers, such as banking, finance or accountancy. There are management training opportunities in large companies and organisations, including the Civil Service, and some openings in the financial departments of companies and local authorities. Careers in buying, marketing and selling, law and insurance are also popular.

Sources of information

Government Economic Service
www.gov.uk/government/organisations/civil-service-government-economic-service

www.whystudyeconomics.ac.uk

www.economist.com

www.neweconomics.org/

'The placement year has really helped me with my career, you can't beat practical experience.'
Chris, BSc Economics

ELECTRONICS

Electronics touches every part of our lives from TVs, mobile phones, cars and our heating control systems right through to transport and defence systems. Electronics is all about practical problem solving and creativity. This course will help you to understand engineering principles and their applications, and gain skills and knowledge of the industry and the many routes available into careers and further or higher education. You will need a good grasp of maths for this course.

The new specifications are designed to give students the electronic and mathematical knowledge and electronic engineering skills to solve problems. They enable students to appreciate how many problems in society can be tackled by the application of the scientific ideas in the field of electronics using engineering processes.

What do you study?

The topics listed give an idea of what could be covered. The exact content of specifications differs according to exam boards. You will need to check with your school or college about the exact options available to you.

➤ **Principles of electronics** – semiconductor components, logic systems, operational amplifiers, signal conversion, AC circuits and passive filters, communications systems, wireless transmission and. instrumentation systems.

➤ **Application of electronics** – timing circuits, sequential logic systems, microcontrollers, digital communications, optical communication, mains power supply systems, high power switching systems and audio systems.

The course reflects up-to-date practice, encourages a safe approach to using electronic systems, and promotes an awareness of the social, economic and cultural impact of electronics. You look at of new and emerging technologies. Computing, such as the use of CAD systems, is also a feature of the course.

20% of the examination marks will be assessed through practical work and you work on tasks and projects to demonstrate that you can analyse problems, and design, build, test and evaluate electronic systems to a set brief.

Subject combinations

Mathematics, physics and computer science A levels would go well and be useful for applications for engineering courses at higher education level; design and technology would also be helpful.

Higher education options

Degree-level study

Don't just research electronic engineering as there are degrees in related disciplines such as computer systems engineering, communications engineering and software engineering. There are also specialist courses such as medical electronics. Most courses lead to a BEng or MEng degree. MEng courses are for the most able students who want a route into fast-track management or research. Many courses have the opportunity for a sandwich year or an industrial placement in the UK, and sometimes abroad.

Degree subject combinations

Electronic engineering can be combined with other branches of engineering such as electrical, and also with subjects such as computer science, languages and business management as well as sciences.

Other higher education qualifications

There are foundation degrees in electronic and electrical engineering, electrotechnical industries, marine technologies, electronics and communications and electrical technology as well as in general engineering and other branches of engineering such as civil engineering. There are HNDS/HNCs in electrical and electronic engineering.

Relevance to other subjects?

Electronics A level gives you useful transferable skills so you could consider many other courses. You will need to check that you have the right A level subject combination for entry – maths may be required, for example. Possible degree subjects might include mechatronics and robotic systems, disaster management, fire risk engineering and computing (mobile).

Important advice

Please note that A level maths and often A level physics (or equivalent) are required for electronics degree courses, although some institutions offer foundation courses in these subjects for those who have not studies those subjects at A level. Some electronics specifications overlap slightly with physics so check with your school or college.

Future careers

After A levels

Many electronics students progress to higher level study but there are technician level jobs at this level, which offer training combining work experience with further study, often through an Advanced Level Apprenticeship. Higher and Degree Apprenticeships offer the opportunity to study up to HNC, HND or degree level.

Typical jobs you might enter as a trainee or apprentice are:

➢ **draftsperson/CAD operator** – drafting plans and documents, using computer technology

➢ **estimator** – working out how much it will cost to design and make a product

➢ **quality assurance technician** – making sure that the product meets the specified quality standards

➢ **inspector** – making sure that everything is running as it should

➢ **planner** – scheduling everyone else's work

➢ **laboratory technician** – helping with research and testing, sometimes at supervisory level

➢ **technician** – helping to develop new ideas and working with other departments in your organisation.

After a degree

Working in electronics

Areas where electronic engineers are recruited include communications, power suppliers, defence, computing and medical electronics.

Most electronics graduates enter graduate trainee schemes with companies. These are the areas of work you could consider:

- design, development and research engineering
- production engineering
- control engineering
- quality assurance engineering
- sales and marketing
- management.

Once in employment as a trainee, you will undertake professional training towards registration as an incorporated or a chartered engineer.

Some companies offer sponsorship for engineering degrees so you would be working for them while you are studying, including during vacations.

Working outside electronics

Your degree will provide you with good problem-solving skills as well as a good scientific and maths grounding, so you could consider trainee schemes in many areas including accountancy, banking and retail.

Sources of information

The Institution of Engineering and Technology
www.theiet.org

The Institute of Physics and Engineering in Medicine
www.ipem.ac.uk

www.btplc.com/careercentre

'If you are creative and want to travel, then engineering has it all.'
Davina, electronics engineer

ENGLISH LANGUAGE

The study of English language at A level gives you the skills to analyse and evaluate written and spoken English and will improve your communication skills. Language is essential to our daily lives: it helps us to understand who we are, and what others might think of us; it is also a way to express thoughts and feelings; it even shapes our view of the world. If you study English language at A level, you develop your knowledge and understanding of the ways in which the English language can help us to communicate, how and why it is used differently by different speakers – and by the same speaker in different situations – and how it has changed over time and is still changing today. Think about the new words or phrases that didn't exist a few years ago such as coasteering and selfie.

What do you study?

The topics listed give an idea of what could be covered. The exact content of specifications differs according to exam boards. You will need to check with your school or college about the exact options available to you.

English language looks at the following:

➤ **a detailed study of the language** – grammar, sentence and word structure; phonetics, phonology and prosodics: how speech sounds and effects are articulated and analysed); graphology: the visual aspects of textual design and appearance; lexis and semantics: the vocabulary of English, including social and historical variations; grammar, including morphology: the structural patterns and shapes of English at sentence, clause, phrase and word level.

➤ **language analysis** – how to unpick a sentence into basic constituents; language development, variation and change through the ages from early-modern English Middle Ages) to the present day.

➤ **different theories and research** – for example, there are three different theories as to how children acquire language and you will have a chance to see how these theories fit in with the latest thinking.

➤ **the social aspects of language** – dialects and the difference between male and female language use.

➤ **language and the media** – the theories behind this; you will study various types of media including newspapers and adverts.

➤ **language variation** – how language has changed over time; how individuals speak English differently, through accent and dialect; how we all vary the language we use according to the situation that we are in or to whom we are talking; historical, geographical, social and individual varieties of English.

➢ **language and identity** – how is language evolving with the introduction of new words? Has English been affected by different migrant communities in the UK? How has English evolved in other English-speaking countries?

➢ **language and representation** – the philosophy of language, e.g. gender and politics. This will cover political correctness, including slang, jargon and taboo language, and occupational usage such as in teaching, building or journalism

➢ **writing for specific genres, audiences and purposes** – you will demonstrate your skill in writing and explore the techniques of a variety of genres in order to produce effective texts for specific genres, audiences and purposes.

Exams are analysis of texts, plus essays. The coursework is 20% of the A level mark and consists of a language investigation and a piece of original writing and commentary.

Most students who take English language A level will have done both English language and literature at GCSE. A modern language at GCSE is useful. Good grades are necessary in order to study at A level.

You must read widely beyond the textbooks and develop a keen ear for eavesdropping on other people's conversations or listening intently to conversations that you have. This latter skill is particularly useful in the part of the course that deals with the spoken word.

N.B. There is also an A level in English language and literature (see the end of the English literature entry for more details).

Subject combinations

If you are thinking of going on to study English language at a higher level, a modern language would be a good subject to combine with A level English. It means that you have a basis for comparison with what you read. If you are thinking of studying linguistics, a modern or classical language (or even two) is almost essential. Subjects that combine well with and support English include history, philosophy, sociology, psychology and media studies. If you are considering an English literature degree, you should look at English language and literature A level or English literature at A level, as English language A level alone may not be accepted.

Higher education options

An A level in English language is often required for degree courses in the subject.

Degree-level study

In practice, an English language degree is often a degree in English language and linguistics. This means that you study linguistics in general and the linguistics of English in particular.

English language degrees will give you a strong understanding of the fundamentals of the English language and the necessary skills to carry out independent research. It also provides you with the knowledge of the historical development of English language as well as the essential understanding of the correlation between language and identity, language variation and language attitudes, language and ideologies, and the role of language in social relations and practices.

You will study the structure and use of geographical, social and historical varieties of English; data collection and analysis; critical skills in examining how language and discourses are represented in the world around us; awareness of language choices we make and the importance of the cultural, literary and historical contexts in which various discourses and texts are produced, and the use of language in business and the media.

Many courses give you the opportunity to apply what you have learned through practical projects focusing on presentation skills and writing for a particular brief, for example writing a press release, speaking to camera or organising a formal business meeting. Some English language degrees offer a placement year, either working or studying abroad.

There are degrees available combining English language and literature and specialising in creative writing. Both English language and literature can be studied for a BEd degree, in which you study education and gain a teaching qualification alongside your English work. There are also courses and options on degrees in teaching English as a foreign language (TEFL) or teaching English as a second language (TESOL).

Degree subject combinations

English language can be combined with many subjects. A combination with English is useful for any subject that requires an ability to understand how language can be used to communicate images, thoughts, emotions and a sense of the society in which the text was written. The most widely available combinations are communication, history, modern languages and sociology.

Other higher education qualifications

There are some foundation degrees where English language could be useful including creative and professional writing, journalism, media practice, interactive media development, sports journalism and broadcast journalism.

There are HND and HNC courses available in media and communication, and creative media-journalism.

There are also pre-entry courses for journalism such as the Foundation Certificate in Journalism, which require good A levels or equivalent and sitting the National Council for the Training of Journalists (NCTJ) entrance test.

Relevance to other subjects?

The study of English language at A level develops skills that will help you in subjects at a higher level. Among these are history, media studies, film studies, drama and linguistics. More applied courses such as creative writing, teaching and journalism are worth investigating.

Important advice

Start taking an interest in English language in its written and spoken form. Look closely at newspaper headlines in different newspapers. Start listening more closely to conversations to hear how people really communicate. Think about the way that you communicate with your friends. How much slang do you use? Do you talk in text speak?

Future careers

After A levels

Studying for A level English language gives you plenty of practice in communicating in both speech and writing, which is an essential skill valued by many employers. You could consider a wide range of administration jobs. It might be useful to gain extra skills in administration, IT or business studies and you could consider taking a full- or part-time course at college. You will find that some companies offer training schemes and apprenticeships, there are now Level 3 apprenticeships in journalism and Higher Apprenticeships in social media and digital marketing. Other possible job areas include retail, marketing and sales.

After a degree

Working in English language

Studying English language and linguistics equips you with skills that are relevant to a wide range of careers. There are many professions that require specific linguistic expertise, for example, publishing, journalism, public relations, advertising copywriting and technical authorship. You could also consider teaching in the UK and abroad, although you might have to do some further training. The ability to 'think linguistically' is of great value to software developers and programmers and communications experts. English language and linguistics graduates are seen by employers as literate, numerate and articulate; studying English fosters skills in analysing and summarising data, arguing effectively and with supporting evidence, thinking logically, strategically and critically, working both independently and as part of a team, meeting deadlines and using computer technology.

Some English language graduates undertake further study in related subjects like linguistics, creative writing, publishing or speech therapy or study for a PGCE for teaching. (See also the English literature section.)

Working outside English language

You will have learned excellent communication skills on your course and a good understanding of the way that different people communicate. These skills can be useful in many types of work and you could consider careers in sales, the media, law, IT, accountancy and finance, management, HR, retail and administration. For some of these careers there are postgraduate diplomas available, such as HR, information science, management and marketing.

Sources of information

Creative Skillset
www.creativeskillset.org

Professional Publishers Association
www.ppa.co.uk

www.bl.uk/soundsfamiliar

National Council for the Training of Journalists (NCTJ)
www.nctj.com

'You usually speak without thinking much about it, but this course helps you to listen and really understand what different people are saying and to really 'understand' what they mean.'
Ellis, taking A levels in English language, law and business

ENGLISH LITERATURE

You need to love reading to study this course but it's not just reading for the sake of it. This course develops your ability to discuss ideas, argue points of view and understand how literature affects and reflects our lives.

You study a wide range of works of literature. You will study prose, poetry and drama and examine the techniques writers use to build characters, create atmosphere, drama or tension, and develop themes and ideas. You will learn to read in a way that will help you to evaluate not just the set texts but any piece of writing. You will learn to develop and express your own opinions. You'll be able to read types of literature you've never read before or look at familiar pieces in a new, more analytical way.

There is also an A level in English language and literature (see the end of this entry for details).

What do you study?

The topics listed give an idea of what could be covered. The exact content of specifications differs according to exam boards. You will need to check with your school or college about the exact options available to you.

The revised specifications recommend a minimum of eight texts, which must include three pre-1900 works including a Shakespeare play, and a post-2000 work. Prose, drama and poetry must all be included.

Set texts come from a wide range of periods and include authors such as Jane Austen, Charlotte Bronte, George Eliot, Thomas Hardy, Kate Chopin and Ian McEwan. Poetry could include works by poets ranging from Chaucer, Coleridge and Keats to Sylvia Plath, Ted Hughes, Carol Anne Duffy and Owen Sheers. Drama might include Congreve, Ibsen, Goldsmith, and Wilde to Caryl Churchill, Peter Whelan, Ben Elton and Richard Curtis.

Some specifications allow you to study on the basis of periods, such as 'World War I' or 'Literature from 1945 to the present day', or cover a whole genre such as 'Love through the ages'.

Some specifications include a comparative and contextual study which will enable you to compare works on a particular theme or from a particular period for example, 1984 by George Orwell and The Handmaid's Tale by Margaret Atwood (Dystopia theme) or The Great Gatsby by F.Scott Fitzgerald and The Grapes of Wrath by John Steinbeck (American literature 1880–1940).

The non-exam part of the A level assessment offers the opportunity for individual research and study and students study and compare texts from either different time periods or themes or from across poetry, drama and prose. This enables students to undertake personal study and research in an area of interest which is a great preparation for higher level study. This forms 20% of the A level marks.

A level English literature involves a lot of reading. You will need to know the texts inside out if you are to do well. You must 'read around your texts', which means read other texts that are related in some way to those you are studying, whether in terms of the themes covered, when they were written or because they were written by the same author. When you study plays for English literature, it is important to remember that they were originally meant to be performed so that must be taken into account in your reading and interpretation.

You will usually take part in readings of the texts you are studying in class. You must take every opportunity to go to the theatre and to watch films and plays of literature. Don't wait for a trip to be organised, try to see as many productions and performances as you can (and not just of your set plays!).

Most students who take English literature A level will have taken both English language and literature at GCSE. Good GCSE grades are necessary in order to study the subject at A level.

Subject combinations

English literature combines well with most subjects and popular combinations include history, philosophy, media studies, sociology, psychology, religious studies, drama and theatre studies, and modern languages. If you are thinking of studying linguistics, a modern or classical language is very useful. Don't forget there is a need for literate scientists so English literature could go well with sciences.

Higher education options

An A level in English literature is often required for degree courses in the subject.

Degree-level study

English literature degrees are flexible and wide ranging. They cover not only traditional areas (like Shakespeare or Dickens) but broader fields such as American literature, creative writing, postcolonial literature and developments in literary theory. Courses could include topics such as crime fiction, literature and addiction, women writers, writing in multicultural Britain, the literature of food or children's literature. Some courses include popular fiction, song lyrics or film. Some courses provide the chance to pursue creative projects in art, film, creative writing and digital media.

Some degrees will include the study of Old English language and literature (also known as Anglo-Saxon). This is very different from modern English and is learned as a foreign language. Other courses have a particular emphasis and can include, for example, study in North America, creative writing or English literature with English language. Both English language and literature can be studied for a BEd degree or as a BA with qualified teacher status (QTS), where you study education and gain a teaching qualification alongside your English work.

Degree subject combinations

English literature combines with related subjects, like journalism, media studies, creative writing and specialisms within English literature, such as American literature. Other popular combinations are history, modern and classical languages, and sociology, as well as more unusual ones including criminology, chemistry and computer science.

Other higher education qualifications

There are no pure English literature foundation degrees but there are related degrees such as English studies, media production, and journalism.

There are no English literature HNDs or HNCs but look at courses like creative media production, media and communication and journalism. There are also foundation journalism courses, run by the National Council for the Training of Journalists (NCTJ).

Relevance to other subjects?

English literature A level develops skills that make a good background for many subjects at a higher level including history, sociology, religious studies, media studies, film studies, drama and linguistics. Consider courses in American studies, communication studies and creative writing.

Important advice

If you apply for an English literature degree one of the common interview questions is: 'What have you read apart from your set texts?' You should try to get into the habit of reading as much as possible in your spare time. Sunday newspapers contain book review sections, which will help you keep in touch with new books and writers. You could also read the Times Literary Supplement or London Review of Books – available online or in your local library.

Future careers

After A levels

A level English literature develops communication skills in both speech and writing, which are valuable in the job market. You could consider sales, marketing, HR or administration jobs. There are apprenticeships available; Advanced Level Apprenticeships in journalism and Higher Apprenticeships in broadcast production and technology, public relations and social media. If you want to work with books and literature, look at library or bookshop work or you could work in admin for a publisher. For all these jobs you will be in competition with graduates, so you should look for opportunities for further training or take an office or business course to help you get in.

After a degree

Working in English

English graduates have a wide range of careers open to them.

➤ **Teaching** – train to teach in schools, colleges or as a TEFL teacher (teaching English as a foreign language) – English is taught at both primary and secondary levels. Postgraduate training is necessary for this.

➤ **Publishing** – be prepared to take any job in publishing and work your way up. Opportunities include copy-editing (checking a manuscript for accuracy, consistency and conformity with the publisher's 'house style') or working as a researcher for non-fiction publications. Don't forget that there are now opportunities in digital publishing and e-books. Selling and marketing in publishing can provide good opportunities as can the legal side and publishing rights. There are opportunities in bookselling both in real and virtual shops.

➤ **Advertising, marketing and PR** – jobs such as copywriter, media planner or buyer, marketing assistant or PR officer. Entry could be via a graduate training scheme or by working your way up from a junior job. There are postgraduate courses available in these areas, which could give you an advantage.

➤ **Journalism** – there are opportunities in printed, digital and broadcast journalism. Consider a postgraduate course to give you an advantage. It is essential that you gain experience and can demonstrate your commitment by, for example, working for a student newspaper or radio station, or a hospital radio service. You need to build up a good portfolio of experience and work to help you get in and progress.

> **Other writing** – the number of people who make their living from 'creative' writing (novels, short stories and drama) is very small. Don't be put off, but remember that you will probably have to do your writing in your spare time to start off with. If you have some funds, there is always self-publishing but you will need to market your books to get sales. If you are happy to pursue other forms of writing, you might want to consider technical or non-fiction writing. There are now opportunities for writing on the web and in social media, blogs etc as many companies need full time staff to promote their web presence.

Working outside English

Apart from those entering teaching, most English graduates do not use their knowledge of English literature professionally. However, you will have learned to propose ideas and theories and to think creatively. This can be useful in many careers including law and business (especially in sales and marketing). For many of these careers, further qualifications or training either in or outside work will be necessary.

Sources of information

National Council for the Training of Journalists (NCTJ)
www.nctj.com

Publishers Association
www.publishers.org.uk

www.bookcareers.com

'I enjoy analysing writers' use of English: how they make a piece of text sound good and how that reflects meaning. Investigating the use of symbols and meanings throughout plays and other texts is also interesting.'
Shona, A levels in English literature, French and Latin

ENGLISH LANGUAGE AND LITERATURE

In A level English language and literature, there is a strong emphasis on language and how it is used in different communicative situations. You learn to study systematically both written and spoken language by analysing different sorts of texts and transcripts, and by writing your own text and commentaries on the language with which you have created them. You will learn the skills of summarising, editing and recasting written material for practical purposes. In addition, you will study literature from various periods right up to the 21st century in the form of plays, short stories, novels or collections of poems. The new specifications include non-fiction as well as fiction. You will analyse the text and look at the representation of speech as well as exploring the stylistic and thematic issues. You will learn to write fluently and coherently. The non-exam part of the A level assessment forms 20% of the final marks and, depending on the specification, could be an analytical essay comparing different texts, writing a non-fiction original writing piece or a personal investigation that explores a specific technique or theme.

For details of higher education, careers and further information, see the English language and English literature entries.

ENVIRONMENTAL SCIENCE

Studying environmental science will give you the knowledge, understanding and skills to make informed judgements on current environmental issues. It is the study of the environment and the place of human beings within it. You learn the principles that are used to decide how to manage the environment and promote sustainability. You cover not only the scientific concepts that provide a basic understanding of the environment but also the social, economic and political aspects of environmental management.

You investigate how humans affect the world in which they live, and you will learn objective and critical approaches to environmental politics. Issues explored on the course include climate change, nuclear power, air, water and noise pollution, land use, ecosystem and habitat loss, endangered species, over-fishing and sustainability

What do you study?

The topics listed give an idea of what could be covered. The exact content of specifications differs according to exam boards. You will need to check with your school or college about the exact options available to you.

➢ **The living environment** – how the conditions on planet Earth allowed early life to develop and survive and how the presence of life on earth brought about environmental change. Ecosystems and how they interact with each other.

➢ **Life processes in the biosphere** – the ecological relationships between organisms and their abiotic and biotic environment in order to understand conservation problems further and how these may be managed.

➢ **Biodiversity** – the importance of the conservation of biodiversity; resources and how sustainable habitat management strategies can be used to secure future supplies. How humans influence biodiversity by over-exploiting natural resources which may affect the populations of many species; deliberate eradication of predators and competitors; changing the eco-system by drainage, pollution or by habitat destruction for building or mineral extraction.

➢ **Habitat conservation and creation** – different types of habitat such as tropical rainforest, tropical coral reefs, and Antarctica, and how they are created and conserved.

➢ **Species** – different types of species, how they evolved and how they can be threatened. Management of desirable species through release programmes and habitat management. Control of undesirable species through culling/eradication. Trade controls and captive breeding. Wildlife species as pest control agents in for example, agriculture.

> **Legislation and protocols that protect biodiversity, habitats and species** – the Wildlife and Countryside Act (1981). Different designations of protected areas for example, Site of Special Scientific Interest (SSSI).

> **Ecological monitoring** – the development of new technologies for ecological monitoring.

> **Biomimetics** – the imitation of the models, systems and elements of nature for the purpose of solving complex human problems. How features in living organisms can be copied in the development of new structures and materials, such as in vehicle design, buildings, materials, ultrasound diagnosis and new medicines.

> **Genetic resources** – the development of new genes to improve crop genetic characteristics developed from the wild relatives of cultivated crops.

The physical environment

> **How the atmosphere works** – atmospheric gases, water and mineral nutrients and how they are essential for life on Earth

> **Climate** – global climate change; how interconnected natural systems cause environmental change. Greenhouse gases, difficulties monitoring and predicting climate change. Carbon footprints and sustainable development; the ozone layer.

> **Physical resources** – how humans exploit natural resource; the impact of unsustainable exploitation:

> **Management of resources** – for example water: metering, low water-use appliances, greywater use, exploitation of new sources, rainwater catchment, new reservoirs/estuary barrages, unexploited aquifers, inter-basin transfers. Mineral resources; recycling.

> **Sustainable management** – formulating management strategies and plans for sustainable activities interconnected with physical processes. Analysis and evaluation of strategies for sustainable management.

> **Energy resources** – resources such as nuclear power, fossil fuels, renewable energy technologies, energy conservation. Future problems of energy supply and how these may be resolved; alternative sources of energy.

> **Transport energy conservation** – improvements in vehicle and road design; biofuels.

> **Building energy conservation and design** – the development of low energy household appliances.

➢ **Pollution** – the different types of pollutants: oil, domestic and industrial waste, nuclear waste, noise pollution, such as traffic and aircraft noise, industrial and domestic noise. Properties of pollutants to explain why some materials or forms of energy cause environmental damage; the study of atmospheric, aquatic and terrestrial pollutants. Minimising releases; treating effluents and managing the damage caused by pollutants. Developing new pollution control technologies.

➢ **Biological resources and sustainability** – factors controlling human population growth in relation to the demands placed upon the planet's resources and life-support systems. Food production and how it must be managed – sustainably; for example overfishing and environmental problems caused by forestry. Study of sustainability – on local, national and global scales.

Research methods

The new specifications emphasise the importance of scientific research skills needed to collect representative data so that reliable conclusions can be formulated. They also help you develop practical, mathematical and problem-solving skills as they relate to environmental issues and the sustainable use of resources.

Maths

10% of the A level marks in the written exams will assess the use of maths skills as they relate to environmental science. The standard is Level 2 or above so equivalent to the standard of the higher tier GCSE maths.

Environmental science involves classroom work, essay writing, discussions, research and class presentations. You spend time on laboratory experiments, fieldwork, surveys, role-play sessions, environmental impact assessments, cost-benefit analysis, computer modelling and energy audits. You visit relevant sites, which could be a nuclear reactor or nature reserve. You are encouraged to do as much reading around the subject as you can, especially about environmental issues in the news. There is no coursework requirement in the new specifications.

GCSEs that could be useful for A level environmental science include biology and geography and other sciences will be very useful.

Subject combinations

Environmental science combines well with biology, geography, geology and chemistry. If you want to take an environmental course at a higher level, biology and geography may be required or preferred, and, in some cases, chemistry. Maths, further maths, statistics or economics could be useful as data analysis can be an important part of environmental degrees. Some universities specify a pass in the practical element of any sciences taken.

Higher education options

Degree-level study

There are many degrees with the word 'environmental' in their title. The most widely offered are environmental science and environmental studies. These include the topics you will have already studied for A level, although in much greater breadth and depth. They vary in the emphasis they give to basic scientific principles so you must check the course content carefully.

Examples of other environment-related degrees available include disaster management, ecology, conservation and environment, environmental geography and climate change, environmental hazards, marine environmental studies, environmental geography, environmental geoscience, environmental management, planning, environment and development, environmental resource management, geochemistry, environmental chemistry, environmental conservation, environment and planning, natural history, ocean science and global development and sustainability.

Degree titles are not always a reliable guide to content, so you should check carefully before you decide which courses to apply for.

Environmental engineering is another option (you will usually need A level mathematics and physics). This is concerned with engineering techniques for solving environmental problems, such as water resource management, pollution, waste management and land reclamation. It is often combined with civil engineering. Some environmental degrees offer a study year abroad or a sandwich placement.

Degree subject combinations

Environmental science is available in combination with many subjects. Examples are archaeology, business, conservation, earth science, ecology, economics, geography, sustainability and technology,

Other higher education qualifications

You can study foundation degrees in related areas including aquaculture and fisheries science, coastal safety management, conservation and ecology, countryside management and conservation, environmental science (wastes, resources and technology), integrated wildlife conservation, renewable energy technologies, river and coastal engineering and sustainable land based strategies. There are also foundation degrees in public and environmental health.

There are environmental science HNCs or HNDs, most of them designed as vocational training. Examples include animal biology and wildlife conservation, countryside management, environmental management and sustainability and green technology.

Relevance to other subjects?

Environmental science A level is concerned with the interaction between people and their environment, so it has a social science element that would be relevant to subjects such as sociology, history, politics, psychology, economics or law. It would be useful for courses such as countryside or land management or business administration.

Important advice

If you are taking biology, geography or physics, there may be some slight overlap with the environmental science specification so check the course content carefully.

Try to get as much experience as you can if you are planning a career in the environment, such as voluntary work with a local environmental or conservation group.

Future careers

After A levels

Many companies now try to operate in a more sustainable and environmental way and there has been a rise in 'green collar jobs', which are jobs concerned with the environment.

You will usually need further training to make direct use of your environmental science knowledge in a job. There are apprenticeships available in areas such as process operations in energy from waste plants, environment enforcement, environmental health, conservation and land management. You could also look at apprenticeships in agriculture, horticulture and arboriculture. There could also be business and finance apprenticeships working with environmental and conservation organisations. Experience as a volunteer may help you to obtain paid work later.

After a degree

Working in environmental science

➤ **Environmental scientist** – working in a university or large commercial company in research or consultancy; a postgraduate qualification will be useful for this type or work.

➤ **Environmental health** – local authorities employ environmental health officers, whose responsibilities include noise control and food safety inspection (postgraduate courses are available)

➤ **Housing management, surveying and town planning** – you will need additional specialist qualifications.

➤ **Waste management/pollution control** – local authorities and private companies employ environmental scientists as recycling/pollution or waste management professionals.

➤ **Government agencies** – there could be opportunities with the Environment Agency or DEFRA as well as the Health and Safety Executive (HSE).

➤ **Nature conservation/wildlife officer** – working for local authorities or national organisations.

➤ **Environmental organisations** – for example Natural England, the Royal Society for the Protection of Birds and the National Parks. These organisations recruit environmental scientists, as do environmental pressure groups such as Friends of the Earth. There is a lot of competition for jobs in these organisations and factors other than academic qualifications are important. You must be able to demonstrate enthusiasm for the work and a good portfolio of voluntary experience.

➤ **Energy efficiency adviser or installer** – assessing how green houses are or installing green energy technologies in houses and businesses, for example solar panels or water reclamation systems; further training will be required.

Working outside environmental science

The general scientific education you will receive as part of an environmental science degree helps you to develop strong observation, data-recording, interpretation and IT skills, as well as the ability to write high-quality reports on your findings. These skills could help you in many careers such as business and finance, advertising and marketing.

Sources of information

Chartered Institute of Environmental Health
www.cieh.org

Chartered Institute of Ecology and Environmental Management
www.cieem.net

Department for Environment, Food and Rural Affairs (DEFRA)
www.gov.uk/defra

Environment Agency
www.environment-agency.gov.uk

Lantra
www.lantra.co.uk

Natural Environment Research Council
www.nerc.ac.uk

www.brightcrop.org.uk

www.letsrecycle.com

www.environmentjob.co.uk

'I help out with my local nature reserve; we organise events such as 'clean up' days. This was something useful to put on my personal statement and I was able to talk about it at my interview.'
Vincent, environmental science undergraduate

FILM STUDIES

The film studies A level has been developed to explore film from the first silent films up to the present day. You will learn to understand and appreciate how films communicate meaning and entertain us, their social, political context and the industry that produces them. You will develop a critical approach to film.

The course covers the study of British and US films, non-English language films and world cinema, and gives you the opportunity to make your own films and write storyboards and screenplays. You also learn about the technical side of film making, such as cinematography, mise-en-scène, editing and sound.

What do you study?

The topics listed give an idea of what could be covered. The exact content of specifications differs according to exam boards. You will need to check with your school or college about the exact options available to you.

➤   You will study feature-length significant films from the US and Britain as well as non-English language films. This includes independent films, i.e. film outside the main commercial structures of Hollywood and Bollywood.

Films studied will be from a wide range of historical periods: 1930-1960, 1961 to 1990, and 1991 to the present day. You will also cover silent films, experimental films, documentaries and short films.

➤   Apart from learning how to analyse and interpret films critically, you study different aspects of film including global film practice, social, cultural and political aspects, technological contexts and how meaning and audience responses are generated through film.

➤   You will look at movements or stylistic developments in film history, characterised by the significant contribution they made to film aesthetics, such as montage, expressionism, neo-realism or the new wave cinemas of the 1960s.

➤   You examine film form; how the features of a film work and produce meaning. These consist of elements of film such as cinematography, editing, sound, lighting, performance and mise-en-scène (sets, props, costumes etc). The narrative construction of a film, camerawork and direction.

➤   You also study the performances of screen actors and how their performances contribute to the overall meaning of the film. You will look at factors such as the dialogue, non-verbal performances and psychological insights into the characters.

30% of the exam marks are assessed through practical work which is the
production of a short film or screenplay to a set brief together with a storyboard
of a key section. You will also have to write an evaluative analysis of the
production in relation to professionally produced films or screenplays.

There is a film studies GCSE available but you don't need this to take the A
level.

Study includes film screenings and close analysis of sequences from different
films, followed by essays, criticism and case studies. You will be expected to
take an active interest in film outside the classroom and be able to talk about it
knowledgeably and critically.

Subject combinations

If you are considering a degree course in film production or directing, you may
need a portfolio or audition in addition to an interview. A level film studies can
help with this. You could consider taking art and design or photography with
film studies, as they will increase your understanding of how visual images are
put together and how they can communicate different ideas.

Some art and design courses allow you to use film and video as part of the
practical work. English literature helps you to express your ideas on paper and
offer clear criticism of others' work, using evidence from texts to back up your
ideas. Media studies, history or modern languages also combine well.

Creative Skillset has a database of approved courses at further education, degree
and postgraduate level, as well as short technical courses. Go to the Creative
Skillset website for more information.

Higher education options

A level film studies is not necessary for entry to film degrees. Note that for some
of the more practical courses based at colleges of art and design, an Art
Foundation course may be helpful to gain entry.

Degree-level study

Film studies courses take a variety of forms: some focus more on the critical and
historical study of film, others on the practical and technical skills involved in
film making. However, many courses include elements of both. As film studies A
level is not offered by every school or college, most degree courses start from
scratch. You can then often decide on the direction that your own course will
take through your choice of options, which cover specialised areas such as

theoretical and analytical studies, camera techniques (using both film and video), scriptwriting and technical production.

Look out for titles such as film production, film and media production and moving image. You will also find more focused courses like digital production and filmmaking, film practice, film technology and visual effects, screenwriting, special effects for film and television, television production management and wildlife media.

Some film studies degrees now offer a placement abroad.

Degree subject combinations

Film studies can be combined with many subjects, for example, English or a language. Many film studies degrees are already 'combined' degrees, as you study video, television, radio or digital media from a practical and/or theoretical viewpoint. If you are interested in the financial production side of film making you might combine film with business, entrepreneurship or innovation.

Other higher education qualifications

Foundation degrees are available in different aspects of film including creative industries (film and video), digital film production, film and media arts production, film and television production, film and television production technology, film production, film production technology, media make up, prosthetic make-up effects and visual effects production technology. Courses can link into degrees or professional practice courses and some will require a portfolio of work for entry.

There are some HND and HNC courses specifically geared towards film and media. Course titles include creative media production, film making, specialist makeup, special and visual effects for film and television, production design and art direction in the film and television industries and digital film production.

Postgraduate courses are available in film and film making.

Relevance to other subjects?

Film studies A level encourages you to develop observational, critical, written and practical skills. It helps you to look at creative products in detail in the context of the society or culture in which they were made. Film studies can lead to degrees in communication studies, English, American studies, sociology, psychology, and philosophy. It could also help you on drama or performing arts courses.

Important advice

If you are considering a degree in film studies or a related area, start by investigating the exact contact and entry requirements of each course, as they can vary a great deal. Try to find out what sort of jobs their graduates got after the course. Check on the Creative Skillset website that the course is accredited with them (with the Creative Skillset Tick).

Future careers

After A levels

The film industry is competitive but it is possible to get in at a junior level with hard work and a bit of luck. Networking is very important in this industry. There may be administration jobs or you might get in as a 'runner' for a film or television company. Runners help everything to run smoothly and provide a range of support in every area of film production. There are now Advanced Level Apprenticeships available in craft and technical roles in film and TV and Advanced Level Apprenticeships in creative and digital media. Higher apprenticeships are available in broadcast and technology.

You could look at work in an area related to film, such as advertising, distribution (getting films to cinemas around the country) or marketing. Roles available are likely to be as an administrator or general assistant, and if you are good at networking and making useful contacts you may be able to get into other roles from there. There may be apprenticeships available in the business side of film.

After a degree

Working in film or television

You should be prepared to get further training or to start in a junior position and work your way up. Postgraduate study could be an option to enhance your skills. Creative Skillset offers advice on how to get your first job.

Most people earn a low wage, work extremely long and unsociable hours and are on short- term freelance contracts. If you are serious about a career in film you must be prepared to network and make contacts at every opportunity as you really have to build your career yourself. You must be prepared to work as a freelance and be self-employed.

Here are some examples of the types of jobs available to you:

➤ **Production runners or assistants** – help run the producers' and directors' offices, involved in films from planning to post- production. Tasks include booking crews, organising the shipping of equipment and arranging timetables. Could lead to production roles such as script supervisor.

➤ **Assistant directors** – work with the director to carry out many of the practical jobs needed during the production of the film. There are different levels of assistant director: first assistants have the most responsibility and help to maintain the shooting schedule; second, third and fourth assistants work with the first assistant and have decreasing levels of responsibility, carrying out tasks such as calling actors and delivering scripts and messages. This work can lead to the role of director, who takes full responsibility for the production.

➤ **Camera operators** – carry out the director's instructions regarding shot composition and development. Start as trainees.

➤ **Designers** – work in film, television or video and use technical and artistic skills. Work in this area can range from costume and set design to designing the continuity sequences used on screen between programmes. To enter this area, you need additional specialised training, which can often involve a postgraduate course or an apprenticeship.

➤ **Script/screen writers** – work freelance and are commissioned by film or television companies. Writing for the screen is very different from writing a book and a good understanding of film terminology and techniques is needed.

For details of other jobs, visit the Creative Skillset website.

Working outside film or television

Film studies graduates could enter advertising and marketing, journalism, publishing, research and arts administration. They can also get into careers that are open to graduates in any discipline, such as business and finance or retail and management training.

Sources of information

British Film Institute
www.bfi.org.uk

Creative Skillset
www.creativeskillset.org
www.creativeskillset.org/careers

London Film School
www.lfs.org.uk

National Film and Television School
www.nftsfilm-tv.ac.uk

www.bbc.co.uk/careers

http://4talent.channel4.com/

> *'Networking is the key to getting a job, that and being willing to do all sort of odd jobs such as getting in the coffees or delivering things .'*
> Bob, working as a runner after a film studies degree

GEOGRAPHY

Are you interested in the world around you? The world we live in is constantly changing. Think about natural and man-made catastrophes in the news such as flooding, earthquakes and war. Geography allows you to see why and how the world changes. It is multidisciplinary, offering the opportunity to develop a range of skills including investigative, IT, graphical, cartographical and statistical, numerical and research. You study a range of topics covering current major global concerns looking at issues like climate change, population growth and globalisation as well as tsunamis and volcanoes. The course will enhance your understanding of the environment and help you understand some of the pressing environmental, economic and social problems facing the world today. The new specifications emphasise the importance of quantitative methods as well as covering new geospatial technologies such as GIS (geographic information systems).

What do you study?

The topics listed give an idea of what could be covered. The exact content of specifications differs according to exam boards. You will need to check with your school or college about the exact options available to you.

The study of geography is divided between two branches:

➤ **Physical geography** is concerned with the Earth, its physical structure and the processes that take place on its surface, as well as physical hazards such as tornadoes, earthquakes and flooding.

➤ **Human geography** looks at the activities of human beings in their physical settings; it addresses current issues, such as food shortages, war, immigration, population and sustainability.

A core theme at A level is the study of how the two branches of geography interact: the effect that the human and physical worlds have on each other. Contemporary concerns such as climate change and global warming are included in the specifications.

The topics covered include:

Physical geography

➤ **Ecosystems (communities of organisms and their environment)** – vegetation (why particular species of plant grow in particular parts of the world) and soils. The pressures on ecosystems, environmental issues including those relating to biodiversity and sustainability.

➢ **Geomorphology** – the shaping of the Earth's surface by the environment (wind, the oceans, glaciers, etc) through the processes of glacier formation, weathering, erosion and desertification, and plate tectonics.

➢ **Water and carbon cycles** – the physical processes which control the cycling of both water and carbon between land, oceans and the atmosphere.

➢ **Atmospheric systems** – climate and weather, atmospheric pollution and global warming, the implications for human life.

➢ **Earth's life support systems** – importance of water and carbon to life on earth, case studies of tropical rainforest and arctic tundra, change over time, links and interdependence between the cycles.

➢ **Landscape systems** – coastal, glaciates and drylands – the processes that shape these and their reaction to the impact of human culture.

➢ **Exploring oceans** – the complex nature of oceans, how they work and how life is supported, sustainability of ocean resources, climate change and the threat of rising water levels.

Human geography

➢ **Globalisation** – benefits of globalisation in terms of growth, development, integration, stability. Costs of globalisation in terms of inequalities, injustice, conflict and environmental impact.

➢ **Global patterns of disease** – the spread of disease and how diseases do not discriminate in relation to who becomes infected or develops symptoms. The physical and human factors involved in the spread of disease. How we combat the spread of disease.

➢ **Food and food security** – food systems, their impact on the environment, the management of food and how to ensure everybody can have access to food security (the state of having reliable access to a sufficient quantity of affordable, nutritious food.)

➢ **Population and the environment** – global population change, migration, resources and environmental concerns.

➢ **Settlement** – where and how people settle in different parts of the world: the location, character and structure of villages, towns and cities and how they grow, change and decline.

The non-examined assessment takes the form of an independent geographical investigation where students can investigate an area of interest to them. This investigation must be supported by reliable data from various sources.

Fieldwork is an important part of the course and central to much of your work. It involves measuring and collecting good quality data, and using techniques appropriate for recording, analysing and using it. Fieldwork might take place in your local area or further afield, giving you the opportunity to observe and record in a variety of settings and landscapes.

Apart from formal lessons, you will take part in classroom discussions and debates .You will learn how to obtain, record, represent, classify and interpret data of different types from both primary and secondary sources. You will learn how to to analyse maps, statistics, newspaper articles and satellite images and use software to manipulate geographical data.

GCSE geography is not always essential for A level study but most schools and colleges will assume some background knowledge. In the new specifications there is an emphasis on mathematical skills so a good grade in maths GCSE will be essential.

Subject combinations

Geography is a subject that falls neatly between the arts and the sciences and combines well with many subjects. The scientific nature of geography, especially physical geography, means that there is a useful overlap with biology, physics, environmental science and geology. You should check this if you have a particular degree course in mind. The human, economic and social aspects of geography go well with A levels such as history, economics, politics and sociology.

Higher education options

Geography is a popular degree and a good grade in A level geography is required for most geography degree courses.

Degree-level study

Geography can be studied for either a BA or BSc degree. The BA concentrates more on human geography and the BSc more on the physical aspects of the subject. A BA might include topics such as population studies, settlement, and distribution of wealth and resources. A BSc course is more likely to involve topics such as geoscience (the scientific study of the structure of the Earth and issues relating to natural resources), hydrology (the study of the movement, distribution, and quality of water), and geomorphology (the study of the origin and evolution of the earth's landforms, both on the continents and within the ocean basins). However, many universities allow for flexibility in choosing topics from both types of degree. Fieldwork is an essential part of geography degrees and may include overseas trips. You may wish to consider more specialised geography courses such as human or physical geography or degrees covering a specific area such as geographic information science), marine and coastal geography, environmental geography, and environment, society and sustainability.

Your first year on a geography course is likely to cover some of the topics you began at A level. However, its scope will extend to urban and rural studies, biogeography, and economic geography and development studies. There will then be specialised options such as medical geography (the characteristics of illness and disease in relation to where they occur), cartography and environmental monitoring, and impact assessment. There are specialised degrees in related subjects such as environmental hazards and disaster management, and emergency and disaster management.

Degree subject combinations

Geography can be combined with one or more of many other subjects. Popular choices include economics, English, history, languages, mathematics and sociology. Biology, IT and environmental science are also possibilities.

Other higher education qualifications

There are foundation degrees available in geography and society, and geography and the environment as well as some related courses in marine conservation and conservation and ecology.

HND and HNC courses are available in marine and coastal geography and also in environmental conservation.

Relevance to other subjects?

Geography A level can be used as a foundation for a wide range of other subjects, such as law, politics, economics, architecture, business studies and anthropology. It is useful for land-based industry courses. It would also be valuable preparation for degrees in environmental science, ecology, surveying, conservation, geology, travel and tourism, and any course that has an international dimension to it like European studies. Landscape architecture, meteorology, oceanography and planning are other possibilities.

Important advice

You will need to examine course content carefully to find out which courses will be suitable for you. A geography degree can be useful for getting into environmental and conservation work. If considering this, it is important to build up a portfolio of voluntary and work experience in conservation before applying. This could be anything from helping to clean up a park at weekends through to a gap year spent in conservation work abroad or in the UK.

Future careers

After A levels

The skills you will have learned on your course, like data handling, team working and IT plus an interest in the world around you, will be useful in all sorts of jobs such as business administration, insurance, retail, finance, media, and travel and tourism. Higher Apprenticeships are available in sustainable resource operations and management, concerned with recycling and waste management.

After a degree

Working in geography

A geography degree will give you many useful skills such as the ability to undertake research and analysis and to interpret data of all types. You will also be numerate with a good knowledge of global issues and the environment. There is a wide range of careers you could consider, although some will need extra study or training.

➢ **Environment and sustainability** – environmental campaigners, recycling officers, cycle route planners, environmental impact officers or disaster managers.

➢ **Planning** – surveying, town planning, landscape architecture, working for local or national government or in industry.

➢ **Mapping** – geographic information systems (GIS), cartography, aerial surveying and remote sensing.

➢ **Science and conservation** – jobs in hazard prediction and management, coastal engineer, flood protection officer, pollution analyst, meteorologist.

- ➢ **Travel and tourism** – travel agent, expedition leader, eco-tour guide.

- ➢ **Development** – aid worker, policy adviser.

- ➢ **Logistics and distribution** – logistics manager, transport manager.

Postgraduate study
Around 20% of geography graduates continue their studies in areas such as environmental management, global security, meteorology, planning and teaching.

Working outside geography
Geography gives you many skills that could be applied to lots of different careers. There are opportunities in local government such as in leisure, recreation and housing management. Having a numerate degree could get you into finance and banking, management training, marketing, advertising and the Civil Service.

Sources of information

Ordnance Survey
www.ordnancesurvey.co.uk

Royal Geographical Society
www.rgs.org

www.geography-site.co.uk

Royal Meteorological Society
www.rmets.org

> 'Geography is not only up-to-date and relevant; it is one of the most exciting, adventurous and valuable subjects to study today. So many of the world's current problems boil down to geography, and need the geographers of the future to help us understand them.'
> Michael Palin, broadcaster

GEOLOGY

Geology (also known as geoscience or earth science) is a branch of science concerned with the structure, evolution and dynamics of the Earth, and with the exploitation of the mineral and energy resources that it contains. Geology is a huge area of study with many specialisms, which overlaps with other sciences, maths and engineering.

If you have a science or geographical background, or just an interest in the planet Earth, geology offers a wide range of topical subjects .The new specifications are designed to give you a scientific understanding of the Earth, its evolution and its sustainable development.

What do you study?

The topics listed give an idea of what could be covered. The exact content of specifications differs according to exam boards. You will need to check with your school or college about the exact options available to you.

Your core study covers:
- elements, minerals and rocks
- the geological structure of the earth
- global tectonics
- surface processes: sedimentary environments and sedimentary rocks
- internal processes: igneous and metamorphic rocks
- evolution of the Earth
- earth materials and resources.

There are also options in:
planetary geology, the lithosphere, the stratigraphy of the British Isles, quaternary geology, geohazards , basin analysis and critical Resources .The critical resources option allows you to investigate the impacts of increased water demand, fossil fuel reserves, such as shale gas, shale oil and coal bed methane, geothermal energy resources in the British Isles and their potential use for ground source heat and cooling, mining and quarrying, extraction technology and the environmental impact of geological factors, extraction planning, and the national and local economic benefits.

There will be fieldwork at home or abroad, including virtual fieldwork. You will also develop your problem-solving skills, learn the application of scientific applications and practices, be able to apply maths in practical contexts and learn how to use technical equipment for investigating, measuring and recording purposes. There is an increased emphasis on technical skills and the use of maths in the new specifications.

Subject combinations

Geology combines well with maths, environmental science, physics, chemistry or biology. If you are considering a degree in geology, A levels are often requested from geography, biology, chemistry, physics, mathematics, further mathematics, statistics, electronics and psychology. If you are offering geography A level as well as geology, check to see if both are acceptable. Science GCSEs and GCSE maths and English are required for further study. A level geology is not normally required for degree-level entry to geology as it is not offered in all schools and colleges.

Higher education options

Degree-level study

If you search for geology degrees, you will find some have titles of earth science or geoscience. The field of geology has expanded a great deal and covers topics geologists of the past never contemplated. This includes overseeing remediation of polluted sites, studying the causes and effects of climate change and advising on wastes and resources.

Geology courses are practical, hands-on degrees that involve a high level of fieldwork on top of thorough academic study. You will explore the Earth and its evolution as a global-scale system, developing an understanding of the role of geology in our environment and communities and its place in multidisciplinary topics such as oceanography, the assessment of natural hazards, and climate change.

There are courses in applied geology, and some that are more specialist such as digital geoscience, engineering geology, environmental geology or geoscience, exploration and resource geology, geological oceanography and minerals management.

Check that courses are accredited by The Geological Society for the purpose of partially meeting the experience requirement for a Chartered Geologist, especially if you are considering becoming a professional geologist. There are MGeol/MSci degrees which are four year undergraduate or integrated masters degrees. These courses are good preparation if you anticipate continuing your education with a PhD/DPhil, but should not be confused with an applied postgraduate masters (MSc), which is often required for a career in the geological industry. Many degrees offer a placement abroad.

Degree subject combinations

Geology/geoscience and earth science combine well with many related subjects, for example, chemistry, physics, geography, biology, ocean science, environmental hazards and petroleum geology, but you will also find combinations with unrelated subjects such as American studies, archaeology and business management.

Other higher education qualifications

There are no geology foundation degrees, but there are related degrees such as subsea engineering and public safety, disaster management and resilience, international mineral extractives technology and clay technology. The HND in chemical engineering at London South Bank University allows progression to a BEng in petroleum engineering.

Relevance to other subjects?

Geology A level can be used as a foundation for science-based careers and courses in environmental science, conservation and land-based industry courses. Environmental hazards and disaster management are other possibilities.

Important advice

Decide whether you want to study a traditional geology degree or go for a degree in earth science or geoscience. These are often broader in scope and may include other subjects linked to the Earth, alongside those focused on the rocks. It is essential that you research courses carefully.

Future careers

After A levels

There are opportunities for geotechnical technicians in a variety of sectors including oil and gas, engineering, the water industry and construction There are Higher Apprenticeships in minerals product technology. You will have skills in researching and interpreting data as well as good numerate skills so you could consider careers in finance and business administration.

After a degree

Working in geology

There are many opportunities in the mining or oil industries, hydrogeology, waste disposal, pollution control or environmental protection. You could become a geologist, an engineering geologist, , carry out research or go into teaching.

Geology/geoscience graduates are needed more than ever as modern society demands increasing amounts of energy, raw materials and other resources such as water, the vast majority of which are discovered by geoscientists, and this is likely to continue into the foreseeable future.

Geoscientists are also needed for civil engineering in designing foundations and tunnels and in environmental projects such as carbon dioxide sequestration.

More than half of geology graduates are in work six months after graduating, with around one in ten working as geologists and mineralogists. Around a quarter enter postgraduate study, either undertaking research or specialising in a particular area of geology.

Working outside geology

Your degree is numerate so it opens up a range of careers in areas such as IT, business and finance. Your science training could be transferred to jobs in the environment, conservation and in land-based industries.

Sources of information

British Geological Survey
www.bgs.ac.uk

The Geological Society
www.geolsoc.org.uk
http://www.geolsoc.org.uk/careers

> *'I've developed a range of skills during my time here such as team work and geological mapping, and enhanced both my analytical and communication skills.'*
> Sadeep, BSc environmental geography

GREEK (classical) / LATIN

These subjects give you the opportunity to learn the ancient Greek and Latin languages (ancient Greek is known as classical Greek) and to study a selection of Greek and Roman literature. The cultures of ancient Greece and Rome are fascinating to study in themselves, and are also the foundation of modern Western civilisations and cultures.

By studying Greek or Latin, you begin to appreciate the language and literature, history and society of the classical world and begin to understand how it has influenced our own. Studying classical languages also trains you in logical and analytical skills as well as providing a foundation for studying a modern language and English.

What do you study?

The topics listed give an idea of what could be covered. The exact content of specifications differs according to exam boards. You will need to check with your school or college about the exact options available to you.

➢ **Knowledge and understanding of the language** – learning the language skills to enable you to read both prose and verse texts in the original language, translating passages taken from the set texts as well as 'unseen' passages of Greek or Latin into English. You carry out comprehension exercises similar to those you are used to in modern languages, and translate English texts into Latin or Greek.

➢ **Literary knowledge and understanding** – looking at how characters, thoughts, actions and situations are presented in Greek or Latin texts, how meanings are conveyed, whether directly or indirectly, and how the texts can be understood in their social, cultural and historical settings. You will read some texts in translation.

➢ **Literary criticism and personal response** – considering the choice and arrangement of words, their rhythm and how the moods they convey are exploited in Greek and Latin literature, and how to think about and explain your own response to the text. The texts studied include those written by Homer, Lysias, Xenophon, Plato, Aristophanes, Euripides, Sophocles, Herodotus or Thucydides (for Greek) or Horace, Catullus Cicero, Ovid, Propertius, Tibullus, Apuleius, Seneca, Virgil or Tacitus (for Latin).

The new specifications are designed to focus on analytical and evaluative skills and cover a range of related subjects such as history, philosophy, religion and politics as well as literature. There is no coursework requirement.

Most people taking A level Latin will already have taken it at GCSE, but many take A level classical Greek as beginners.

Latin and ancient Greek stopped being everyday languages long ago. You cannot learn to speak them, or listen to the spoken language, as you do with a modern language. Instead, you work through reading and writing.

Classes concentrate on grammatical analysis, understanding, analysing and appreciating the literary qualities of the set texts and translation. However, the teaching of classical languages has gained from developments in modern language teaching, so it is not as different as you might expect. You may go on visits to museums or sites with links to the classics.

Subject combinations

If you are looking at a degree in Latin or Greek and have the opportunity to take the language for A level, then you should. If you are thinking of studying both languages at university, you don't have to offer classical Greek A level as well, but a modern language alongside Latin would be helpful. Greek combines well with most A levels including history, modern languages or English. If you are considering a degree in archaeology then mathematics or a science, especially chemistry, would be useful as archaeology uses scientific techniques for the analysis of archaeological sites and remains. If you are considering medicine then plenty of anatomy and pathology terms are in Greek or Latin so either could be a useful subject along with your sciences.

Higher education options

As the opportunity to study Latin or classical Greek is not always available in schools, some universities now teach them from scratch offering different routes to beginners and those with the A level .

For classics degrees (Latin and Greek), you usually have to offer one or both of the languages (if only one, Latin is the usual requirement). There are a few classics courses that will accept a GCSE in Greek or Latin.

Degree-level study

The following options are open to you at degree level:

- a single-subject degree in either Latin or Greek (although often you can also study the other language as a minor or through options)
- a degree in classics (Latin and Greek) – again, you can usually vary the proportions of the two languages, or concentrate more on one or the other as you progress through your degree.

In both these types of degree, you will spend much of your time reading Latin or Greek literature, developing your understanding and appreciation of the language. Naturally, the number and variety of writers that you study will expand greatly from your A level work. You may also have the opportunity to study the history of Latin or Greek. Some courses allow you to study the Latin used after the end of the Roman period (about AD 476) up to the Middle Ages (ending about AD 1500). There will be non-linguistic options including classical archaeology, art and architecture and ancient philosophy as well as ancient history and classical literature in translation. Most degree courses are very flexible and allow you to choose the proportion of the time that you wish to devote to each of these topics.

Degree subject combinations

You can combine the study of Latin or Greek with many other subjects especially English, ancient history, archaeology and modern languages, although you will find combinations with computing and economics. Combining the study of a classical language with the modern languages that have developed from it can be very interesting. You can combine classics with modern Greek and with other modern languages like Czech, Dutch, Hebrew, French, Italian and Arabic.

Other higher education qualifications

There are no foundation degrees directly related to Greek and Latin but related subjects available include history and heritage management studies, archaeology and historic landscape conservation and history, heritage and archaeology. There are no HNDs or HNCs in Latin or ancient Greek.

Relevance to other subjects?

The study of classical Greek and/or Latin can lead to many courses at university. It is a foundation for ancient history, classics, classical studies, languages, history, English, law, philosophy and theology.

Even if you don't think that you will want to take Greek or Latin beyond A level, don't rule it out at this stage. Your study of a language rather different from English, the alternative language-learning techniques demanded, and (for Greek) the mastery of a different writing system, provide good evidence of your intellectual abilities. Studying a more unusual subject provides a good talking point at interviews!

Important advice

There is variation and flexibility in the exact texts and periods covered by different classics degree courses and a wide variety of courses in related areas, classical civilisation for example. You must think carefully about exactly which aspects of your studies of Latin or Greek you most enjoy and then find a degree course that fits your interests.

Future careers

After A levels

Latin or Greek A levels are unlikely to lead directly to related work although if you work in law, you will find Latin useful. However, the different disciplines and techniques involved in studying a 'dead' language in a more formal way suggest a clear, logical mind. The study of classical languages will also help you in any language study you might do now or in the future. You could consider careers that are open to anyone with good A levels, such as banking, insurance, accountancy, retail or national or local government. Don't forget to look at Higher Apprenticeships in these areas which could lead to degree level study.

After a degree

Working with Greek or Latin

There are only a few careers in which you can really use Latin or Greek and these, as you might expect, are concerned with passing on your knowledge to others.

➤   **Teaching Latin or Greek in schools** – this is the main option and the independent school sector offers most opportunities. If you are interested in teaching younger age groups (below A level), you would need to offer another subject such as history, religious studies, a modern language or English.

➤   **Teaching in higher education** – this is usually coupled with research and postgraduate study will be necessary.

➤   **Archaeology** – there may be some opportunities for graduates in Latin or Greek to work as archaeologists, discovering and studying the material evidence of early history. The work ranges from organising digs (excavations), through charting out farmland that may have once formed a Roman settlement, to the assembly and treatment of new pieces of evidence in museums. You would need to undertake further training, but work experience can be gained through taking part in digs during vacations or at weekends. Remember that you will be in competition with graduates who have specialist archaeology degrees.

➢ **Library and archive work** – there may be some opportunities in specialist classical libraries or archives. Further training would be required after your degree.

➢ **The heritage industry** – there may be opportunities to work in specialist museums or as tour guides or historic interpreters using your knowledge of Greek or Latin.

Working outside Greek and Latin

Very few classics graduates end up working in a directly related area. However, their skills are respected and valued by employers in other fields. Employers recognise that classics graduates can think clearly and logically and, because of this, careers in HM Revenue and Customs or as tax advisers are an interesting destination for classics graduates.

Classics graduates go into a wide variety of jobs such as research, education, IT, librarianship or museum work, and many go into management and administration, the Civil Service, banking, insurance, advertising, publishing and journalism.

A degree in Latin or Greek would be a good background if you are thinking of a career in law (the study of Roman law is included in many law courses), or you could enter accountancy training at the graduate stage.

Sources of information

www.classicspage.com

www.ancientgreekonline.com

www.latintests.net

> *'Studying classics is still as relevant and interesting now as it was yesterday. This course is both challenging and fascinating so I highly recommend you pursue something you love, like I have.'*
> Simon, Classics undergraduate

HISTORY

'Those who cannot remember the past are condemned to repeat it'
George Santayana (1863-1952)

It is said that we can learn from the past to avoid the same mistakes in the future. The study of history is concerned with when and why things happened and attempts to analyse the significance of past events. The best reason for taking a history course is that the past fascinates you and you enjoy studying it. History combines the excitement of exploration and discovery with the sense of reward that comes from successfully confronting and making sense of complex and challenging problems.

The purpose of historical inquiry is not simply to present facts but to search for an interpretation of the past. Historians attempt to find patterns and establish meaning through the study of evidence. It provides skills and understanding that will be valuable in any career.

What do you study?

The topics listed give an idea of what could be covered. The exact content of specifications differs according to exam boards. You will need to check with your school or college about the exact options available to you.

The revised history A level specifications still require that students study British history and also include non-British history. Students will also be required to study topics from a chronological range of at least 100 years. This is a thematic study.

The A level has a 20% non-exam assessment. The non-exam assessment is a historical enquiry that is independently researched and investigates specific historical questions, problems or issues. The purpose of this coursework is to enable students to develop skills in the analysis and evaluation of interpretations of history in a chosen question, problem or issue as part of an independently researched assignment.

There are a wide variety of history specifications for A level. Options on courses include world history, economic and social, modern and medieval history and there are wide choices available in each specification.

Examples of what you might study for British history:
- Alfred and the making of England 871-1016
- England 1485-1558: the early Tudors
- The early Stuarts and the origins of the Civil War 1603-1660
- The making of Georgian Britain 1687- 1769
- Britain 1930-1997

Examples of what you might study for non-British history:
- The rise of Islam c.550-750
- The crusades and the crusader states 1095-1192
- Russia 1645-1741
- The French Revolution and the rule of Napoleon 1774-1815
- Japan 1814-1937
- The Cold War in Europe 1941-1995
- Apartheid and reconciliation: South African politics 1948-1999.

Examples of the thematic study and historical interpretations:
- The early Anglo-Saxons c.400-800
- The Renaissance c.1400-c.1600
- Popular culture and the witchcraze of the 16th and 17th Centuries
- The challenge of German nationalism 1789-1919
- Britain and Ireland 1791-1921
- Civil rights in the USA 1865-1992
- The Middle East 1908- 2011: Ottomans to Arab Spring.

You don't need to have studied history at GCSE to take the A level. Some degree courses in history require a modern language at GCSE. All history degrees tend to ask for history A level at a specific grade.

History A level involves being able to read and absorb information quickly. There is never enough class time to cover every aspect of every topic, so the more reading you can do on your own the better. Class discussions form an important part of the course but they must be backed up by note-taking and reading. There will also be field study trips to places of historical interest.

Subject combinations

If you want to study history at degree level then the A level is the obvious choice, as it is a requirement for many history degree courses. You will need to develop skills in research analysis and interpretation to study A level history so you might want to choose other subjects that will provide supporting knowledge and skills.

Politics will add to your understanding of political ideology and the British political system, which will be useful if you are studying modern history. Sociology and economics also cover a number of topics relating to developments in the Western world, requiring the ability to research and interpret data critically. A level English will help the development of your assignment-writing skills. You might also want to consider combinations with modern foreign languages or classics.

Higher education options

Degree-level study

There are many history and history-related degree courses. The largest number of courses are in British and European history, although they do not all cover all periods. As at A level, course topics relate either to periods, geographical areas or themes. Some interesting options on courses include the social history of medicine, gender history, the crusades, intellectual and religious history, financial history, the history of technology and industrial relations. You do not have to opt for a degree covering the periods that you studied at A level so you have the opportunity to try something new.

If you are sure that you want to specialise from the start, you could look at degrees in ancient history, economic and social history, American history, medieval studies, military history, peace/war studies, global history or Scottish history. Some modern history courses offer a year studying in Europe and some offer related work experience.

Degree subject combinations

History can be combined with many other subjects. The most widely available are English, geography, languages, philosophy, politics and sociology and there are combinations with less traditional subjects such as sports, new media publishing or digital humanities.

Other higher education qualifications

There are foundation degrees in history and heritage management studies, history with English, archaeology and historic landscape conservation, and history, heritage and archaeology.

There are no HNDs or HNCs in history although there are some courses for which an A level in history would be good preparation. HNDs or HNCs in administration and information technology or business management, for example, would put to good use your experience of collecting and analysing information.

Relevance to other subjects?

Even if you don't continue with your history studies, you will find that A level history is a well-respected qualification for many courses. In degrees like law, modern languages, English, politics, sociology, economics and business you will find opportunities to use your writing and analytical skills.

Important advice

As history is such a popular degree, it would be useful to visit historical places that relate to your studies or interests. These could be historic houses and places such as Quarry Bank Mill in Cheshire, the Potteries Museum in Stoke-on-Trent and Ironbridge Gorge in Shropshire. Do some research into them beforehand so that you know what to look for once you get there. You should be prepared to do a lot of reading in your spare time. The monthly magazine, History Today, will give you a taste of different historical periods and topics before you study them in detail, as will the wide range of historical programmes on TV.

All history degrees at Oxford University require a selection test called the History Aptitude Test (HAT). Check to see if other universities require a selection test.

Future careers

After A levels

The wide range of skills and knowledge that you will develop as a history A level student will be helpful in finding employment. You will be able to think and argue logically, write well and be able to organise and analyse large quantities of information. These are the kinds of skills needed to work in areas such as administration, management, sales and marketing. With further training you might find work in libraries or archives and there are apprenticeships available in library and information work. There could also be apprenticeships in the heritage and cultural sector working with organisations such as the National Trust.

After a degree

Working in history

There are some careers in which you can use your studies directly:

➢ **teaching** – teaching history is the most direct way to use and develop your subject knowledge. To teach in state schools you would need to undertake further training to gain QTS (Qualified Teacher Status) . University lecturing is a possibility after specialised postgraduate study and research in history

➢ **museum work** – work in museums (usually after postgraduate training).

> ➤ **archive work** – archivists are employed either by the Government (in record offices) by the media or industry. Again, further postgraduate training in information management would help your prospects

> ➤ **heritage management** – this could involve a variety of roles in the conservation and management of heritage sites like historic buildings, museums, ancient monuments and other properties.

Working outside history

History graduates work in many areas of management and administration because their eye for detail, research skills and ability to form logical arguments can make them ideal organisers of both people and resources. They also work for local and national government, in finance, marketing, sales and the media. History is often seen as a good preparation for a career in law (shown by the fact that some universities recommend A level history rather than A level law as an entry qualification to law courses).

Sources of information

The Historical Association
www.history.org.uk

Creative Choices heritage careers
www.ccskills.org.uk/careers/advice/job-profiles/heritage

www.spartacus-educational.com

www.historytoday.com

> *'When I was looking for graduate jobs, I wasn't sure how a history degree would help me. I looked at the skills I had gained from my degree and realised that I could organise and analyse things, present to an audience and also argue a case both verbally and in written form. My job now is with a publisher and I analyse information and data relating to finance. I never thought that history would lead to this job.'*
> Charlie, financial analyst with a degree in history

HISTORY OF ART

In history of art A level you study the work of artists, sculptors and architects, from 500BC to the present day. It provides you with a broad knowledge of world civilisations including the works of art and architecture of different cultures, groups and individuals from across the globe. Works are studied in the light of the political, economic, social, religious and cultural context in which they were created. You learn about the artistic tradition in which the artists worked, and study the techniques that are used in painting, sculpture and architecture.

The new specifications offer a broader choice and include not just Western art but global art and architecture. They also place emphasis on developing visual and analytical skills.

What do you study?

The topics listed give an idea of what could be covered. The exact content of specifications differs according to exam boards. You will need to check with your school or college about the exact options available to you.

1. VISUAL ANALYSIS

You learn how to 'look at and interpret' works of art such as painting, sculpture and architecture. How to interpret paintings taking into account such things as composition; colour, light and tone; materials and techniques. How sculpture can vary according to materials, techniques and processes and size and how architecture is influenced by site and location, materials and scale.

2. THEMATIC STUDY

You acquire a knowledge and understanding of historical art themes in relation to examples of works of global art and architecture, artists and architects drawn from classical Greece to the present day. All works of art are studied in relation to a particular theme and you look at each work in the light of these. For A level, you study two themes from four options.

There are prescribed artists/architects/works for each theme and you study two works by each of three artists from the list and you will study at least four additional artists and works for each theme.

For each theme you study:
- **materials, techniques and processes** – how works of art are produced
- **form and style** – how the formal features of art and architecture contribute to its style and meaning and how different styles have evolved

- **form and function** – the purpose and appearance of, for example, a building, and how to evaluate it taking into account its role as a functional building as well as an artistic work
- **historical and** social contexts – how to interpret works of art in the light of history and social history
- **patronage** – what influence artistic patronage has on works of art
- **social and cultural status** – how these influence art
- **gender, nationality and identity** – how styles evolve due to these factors.

The following are the four theme options:

➤ **Nature in art** – This theme covers the ways in which the motifs, messages and materials of nature have been used across time and place.

Prescribed artists/architects/works are Katsushika Hokusai, JMW Turner, Claude Monet, Antoni Gaudí, Georgia O'Keeffe, Richard Long.

➤ **Identities in art** – This theme covers the representation of divine beings, individuals, groups and of communities or nations in 2D, 3D and architecture across time and place. You study the variety and connections in works from across the world.

Prescribed artists/architects/works are Benin bronze plaques, Rembrandt, Christopher Wren, Vincent van Gogh, Frida Kahlo, Chris Ofili.

➤ **War in art** – This theme covers the preparation, participation and responses to international and civil wars in works of 2D and 3D art and in architecture.

Prescribed artists/architects/works are 'Augustus of Prima Porta' and 'Ara Pacis', Red Fort and Agra Fort of Shah Jahan, Francisco Goya, Otto Dix, Käthe Kollwitz, Henry Moore.

➤ **Journeys in art** – This theme explores the responses to spiritual, physical and psychological journeys undertaken by art and artists and their impact on subsequent works of art and architecture.

Prescribed artists/architects/works are Phidias, Albrecht Dürer, Mimar Sinan, Daniel Libeskind, Ai Wei Wei, Sonia Boyce.

3. PERIOD STUDY

The study of a specific period gives you the opportunity to research and explore the key movements, concepts, artists, contextual factors and related developments in a specific place/s and across a clearly-defined time frame.

Two periods are studied from the following five options for A level. Students must research in detail at least three works by each of two artists.

> **Invention and illusion: the Renaissance in Italy (1420-1520)**

Prescribed artists/architects are Masaccio, Donatello, Brunelleschi, Giovanni Bellini, and Michelangelo.

> **Power and persuasion: the Baroque in Catholic Europe (1597-1685)**

This module offers an in-depth study of the art and architecture of the Italian States, France, Spain and the Spanish Netherlands. You explore the impact of religious, historical and philosophical factors on art and its audiences of monarchs, nobility, individuals and groups across the region.

Prescribed artists/architects are Caravaggio, Gian Lorenzo Bernini, Artemisia Gentileschi, Peter Paul Rubens, Diego Velázquez.

> **Rebellion and revival: the avant-garde in Britain and France (1848-1899)**

This option offers the opportunity to explore the works of the Impressionists and Post Impressionists as well as those of the Pre-Raphaelite and Art Nouveau movements in Britain and France. You will look closely at the profound social, political and technological changes of this era and explore and evaluate their impact on artists and their art.

Prescribed artists/architects are John Everett Millais, Édouard Manet, Edgar Degas, Auguste Rodin, Berthe Morisot.

> **Brave new world: Modernism in Europe (1900-1939)**

This option has been designed to offer an in-depth investigation into art and architecture across Britain, France, Spain, Germany, Italy and the Netherlands and the development of art and artists from these countries across from the period of the 1900 International Exhibition in Paris to the outbreak of World War II in 1939.

Prescribed artists/architects are Henri Matisse, Paula Modersohn-Becker, Jacob Epstein, Pablo Picasso, Le Corbusier.

> **Pop life: contemporary art and architecture in Britain and the USA (1960-2015)**

This module explores the relationship between Britain and the USA in art and architecture, and the dynamic nature of responses on both sides of the Atlantic. Students will explore how key artists use their voice in contemporary politics, philosophy and arguments of identity as well as considering the changing role of the gallery and the impact on our environment of architectural creations by Norman Foster and others.

Prescribed artists/architects are Andy Warhol, Norman Foster, Mary Kelly, Yinka Shonibare, Rachel Whiteread.

The course is examined through written exams.

There is no GCSE history of art and you are not expected to know a lot about art history before you start the A level although obviously it will help. You don't have to be good at painting or drawing but it may help you if have experience of art, photography, history, languages, politics or sociology at GCSE. The most important thing is a real interest and enthusiasm for art history.

History of art is based around the detailed study of works of art. You can expect a lot of group work, discussing images of the works, whether they are paintings, sculptures or buildings. There could be study visits to galleries in the UK and possibly in Europe, such as Florence, Paris, Amsterdam or Barcelona.

Subject combinations

If you are thinking of studying history of art at degree level, it is a good idea to combine the A level with subjects that complement your work. Art and design, English, history, classical civilisation or religious studies would provide invaluable background knowledge. Languages (especially French, German or Italian) also combine well. Even if you don't consider yourself 'artistic', you may find history of art a useful accompaniment to other subjects. For example, combining history of art with a science-based subject may not seem an obvious choice but can be a help with careers such as archaeology and art restoration or conservation, which require scientific skills. The history of art A level provides a useful background for an Art Foundation course although you will also need a portfolio of art work for entry.

Higher education options

It is not essential to have studied A level history of art in order to study it at a higher level.

Degree-level study

A history of art degree will extend your studies much further than the Western world.

You may spend some of your time focusing on a single artist or artistic movement, but you will have the opportunity to study topics such as world cinema, photography and the art of other civilisations. Some courses include practical studio work in art or design. Many courses offer a study period abroad, ranging from a week, to a term or a year. Most of these visits are to Europe, although North America and Australia are possibilities. When researching courses look at art history, history of art and design, visual culture, history of art and architectural history. There is also a curatorial studies degree which is for those interested in curating or gallery management and includes hand-on experience in museums and galleries.

Degree subject combinations

History of art is available with related subjects such as fine art and many others such as archaeology, English, film, heritage management, history, museum studies, publishing and languages.

Other higher education qualifications

There are no history of art foundation degrees although there are plenty of art and design courses, some with a module in art history.

There are no HND or HNC subjects in history of art but plenty of practical art courses such as art and design, fine art, graphics and illustration.

There are also art history courses available at postgraduate level. If you are thinking about the practical study of art, you should consider taking an Art Foundation course, which will help you get into a practical design course.

Relevance to other subjects?

The history of art A level will be useful for entry to humanities and social science degrees. Related courses you might consider include architecture, archaeology, furniture design, interior design and art gallery and museum studies.

Important advice

The best preparation for the study of art history at a higher level is to visit as many galleries, museums and churches as you can. Many art collections are now available on the web so you don't have to travel far. Most art galleries are free and you may find some near you.

Future careers

After A levels

If you intend to go into work straight after A level history of art you may find work as a junior assistant in a gallery, auction house, design company or antiques business. You could consider part-time study to further your knowledge in these areas. There may be apprenticeships in these areas of work.

After a degree

Working in history of art

Careers in or related to art history often require further postgraduate study.

Possible careers include:
- museum, gallery or the antiques business
- arts administration or management
- auctioneer or valuer
- picture researcher
- specialist art or architecture librarian/archivist
- work related to the theatre, arts centres and arts sponsorship for large companies, and the arts support schemes run by local authorities and central government
- heritage industries – many tourist attractions, historic houses or industrial archaeology sites have an 'art dimension'
- specialist travel and tourism (e.g. lecturing on art tours)
- art and design publishing, broadcasting and journalism
- conservation and restoration.

Working outside history of art

You will find the skills and knowledge gained on a history of art degree useful for the many careers open to graduates in any subject, such as buying, marketing and selling, finance and administration. Teaching is another option.

Sources of information

Association of Art Historians
www.aah.org.uk

The National Gallery
www.nationalgallery.org.uk

ICON (the Institute of Conservation)
www.icon.org.uk

www.ccskills.org.uk/careers/advice/any/heritage

www.chart.ac.uk/vlib

> *'If you want to get into conservation of any type, make sure you get some sciences, especially chemistry, at either GCSE or A level.'*
> Theresa, taking a postgraduate qualification in fine art restoration after a degree in history of art.

LAW

A level law is designed to enable students to develop an understanding of both public and private law within the legal system of England and Wales. It develops your skills in constructing persuasive legal arguments and evaluating the strength of such arguments. You will develop the ability to think critically about the role of law in society and develop an understanding of legal method and reasoning as used by lawyers and the judiciary.

What do you study?

The topics listed give an idea of what could be covered. The exact content of specifications differs according to exam boards. You will need to check with your school or college about the exact options available to you.

➢ **Nature of law** – covers the study of the distinction between enforceable legal rules and principles and other rules and norms of behaviour; criminal and civil law and the different sources of law (including custom, statutory law and the common law).

You also look at issues such as law and society (including the role law plays in society), law and morality (including the distinction between law and morals; different moral views and the relationship between law and morals and the legal enforcement of moral values; the meaning of justice and theories of justice and the extent to which the law achieves justice.

➢ **The legal system** – the work of barristers, solicitors and legal executives and other legal personnel; the criminal courts and other forms of dispute resolution including civil courts and the appeal system; appeals, sentencing and court powers; the role of lay people within the criminal process; regulation of the legal professions; the judiciary – the role of judges and magistrates; access to justice and funding, both public and private.

- **how the law is made** – Parliamentary law making including Green and White Papers; the legislative process, delegated legislation, statutory interpretation. Law reform including the Law Commission. EU law.
- **legal disputes resolution** – the criminal and civil courts, tribunals, arbitration.
- **the courts** – the hierarchy of the courts including the Supreme Court, the criminal and civil courts, the jury system.

➢ **Private law**

Law of contract
- **the rules and theory** of the law of contract
- **contracts** – formation of contract, contractual terms, invalid contracts, discharge of contract, breach of contract, damages, mitigation of loss
- **consumer protection**.

Law of tort
- **the rules and theory of the law of tort** – this area of law covers the majority of all civil lawsuits. In brief, every claim that arises in civil courts with the exception of contractual disputes falls under tort law. The concept of tort law is to redress a wrong done to a person, usually by awarding them monetary damages as compensation. So it would cover areas like medical negligence, personal injury and include issues of compensation and damages.

➢ **Public law**

Criminal law – the rules and theory in criminal law:
- **the ingredients of an offence** – commission of the physical act, the mental element
- **offences against the person** – fatal offences of murder, voluntary manslaughter and involuntary manslaughter and non-fatal offences of assault, battery, assault occasioning actual bodily harm, wounding and grievous bodily harm with intent
- **offences against property** – theft, robbery, burglary, criminal damage, fraud offences
- **defences** – insanity, intoxication, self-defence, provocation, duress and duress of circumstances
- **other topics** – principles of criminal liability, being an accessory to a crime.

➢ **Human rights law**

- **the rules and theory of human rights law**; protection of the individual's rights and freedoms in the UK including the history of the European Court of Human Rights; the impact of the Human Rights Act 1998.

Legal skills

You develop competence in using legal skills throughout your studies. You will be assessed on your ability to formulate a reasoned, clear, concise and logical legal argument to support a particular proposition, by using the relevant legal rules and principles that support that argument. You must be able use appropriate legal terminology and be able to analyse and critically evaluate legal issues by identifying different perspectives, being able to support their identification of the strongest viewpoint and demonstrating the ability to counter alternative viewpoints.

There is no coursework for law A level. It is assessed through final exams.

You need to be able to write well, think logically and have a good memory. You must be prepared to study and understand a lot of written material. You will also get involved in debating. You will write essays that explore the relevant concepts and analyse them to reach a conclusion. In addition, you have to apply legal principles and cases to hypothetical problems and assess how appropriate they are to their solution. There will be visits to local and regional courts and you might get to visit places like the House of Commons, the Royal Courts of Justice and the Old Bailey.

Subject combinations

The ability to express yourself clearly both orally and in writing is essential for the study and practice of law. You may wish to combine law with English or history to help develop these skills, and these are useful for entry to law degrees as many universities prefer essay-based subjects. Subjects such as business or economics can help you to understand the context in which legal work is carried out. Psychology, sociology and politics can also provide a good foundation for further study in law-related subjects. Sciences can also be useful, especially if you want to specialise in something like intellectual property. A modern foreign language could open up the opportunity to study in another country and even gain a legal qualification there.

Higher education options

An A level or GCSE in law is not essential for study of the subject at university. Some university law departments sometimes prefer students to start their degree course as a beginner in law so you must check this when researching courses. However, students who have studied law at A level can find that it gives them a head start at university.

Note that some universities use the National Admissions Test for Law (LNAT) to help them to select candidates – you can find out more about this at www.lnat.ac.uk Make sure you check out the deadlines for tests.

Degree-level study

Law degrees consist of a core of essential topics, which are those you need to take and pass if you want to obtain the maximum exemption from professional examinations. You will need to check whether a degree is a 'qualifying'' law degree.

A qualifying law degree involves seven foundation subjects which are currently:
- contract
- tort
- constitutional and administrative law
- criminal law
- property law
- equity and trusts
- law of the European Union.

In addition you will study legal skills and methods and have the opportunity to take different options, for example: bioethics, advanced constitutional law, company law, global law, international human rights, UN laws and practices, women and the criminal justice system, youth crime and youth justice, tax law and environmental law.

Some degrees include the legal practice (for solicitors) or Bar exempting courses (for barristers). Some qualifying law degrees specialise in areas such as criminal law, European law, public law, consumer law, human rights, business law or entertainment law. You will find a full list of qualifying law degrees on the Solicitors Regulation Authority website (see further information).

Degree subject combinations

The core topics take up approximately half of your time, so it is sometimes possible to obtain full professional exemptions if you study law in combination with another subject. This is something to check carefully as you plan your UCAS applications. Perhaps the most popular subjects to combine with law are those that provide some complementary experience and therefore broaden your career prospects. Examples are politics, economics, sociology, psychology, languages and business studies. Many law degrees now offer a European or wider international perspective, such as American or Chinese so you would study the law or language of one or more other countries and sometimes both. This is important as increasingly legal practice crosses national boundaries.

Other higher education qualifications

There are many legal and related foundation degrees available, including law, criminology and criminal justice, policing law and investigation, legal studies, and paralegal studies.

There are HNDs and HNCs in subjects such as law, business law, legal studies, business and policing. Such courses are more vocational than degree courses, and can form a good preparation for a legal career outside the main legal professions – as a court or police officer, for example.

Within the legal profession you could go into paralegal jobs, such as a legal executive or secretary, which could eventually lead to part-time study to qualify in law, see section below.

Non-graduate route to law

A degree is not the only way of qualifying in law. It is possible to work up from being a paralegal or legal executive. The Chartered Institute of Legal Executives (ILEX) offer a non-graduate route to qualifying as a solicitor. You do this by working in legal employment and studying part time. There are also apprenticeships, see 'After A levels' section.

Relevance to other subjects?

The law A level develops your ability to think logically, make balanced judgements based upon clear evidence, and understand the social effects and consequences of such judgements. It is a good basis for almost any social science course at a higher level, including sociology, psychology, politics, economics or business studies. Your practice in essay writing and mastering factual information would make you a good candidate for other subjects such as history, geography, English or classics.

Important advice

Take this A level because you are fascinated by the subject not because you are thinking ahead to the career possibilities. If you are considering a career in law consider:
- do you have the academic ability to cope with a demanding course?
- are you able to compete with very able people to win a place?
- will you be able to meet the costs of qualifying?
- do you have a strong interest in and aptitude for the day-to-day work of a solicitor /barrister?

Although law is an academic subject, it requires students to consider the practical effect of the theory by applying it to real-life situations. Go and sit in the public gallery at a local court to appreciate the impact that law has on everyday life. If you can, get some work experience with a law firm or lawyer.

Future careers

After A levels

You won't come away from the law A level as a fully-qualified lawyer. However, the course does provide valuable background knowledge if you want to work for a law firm in a support role and train part time. Legal apprenticeships in England are now available as an alternative to the traditional graduate route to qualification and go up to Level 7. There are also Advanced Level Apprenticeships in legal services.

You could also consider becoming a law costs draftsman; they ensure that a firm's clients are properly charged for work undertaken on the clients' behalf. You usually train on the job over two years. There are also jobs as legal cashiers and legal secretaries. There are also related jobs such as being a court usher or administrative jobs in the courts.

Your law A level would be useful in many business, finance and administrative jobs so you could look at Higher Apprenticeships.

After a degree

Working in law

To specialise within the field of law it is necessary to gain additional qualifications after your degree:

➢ **barristers** – represent their clients in the courts. They must first take the one-year, full-time Bar Professional Training Course (BPTC), followed by a pupillage (apprenticeship) within a set of chambers for at least one more year. Non-law graduates have to study for a Common Professional Examination (CPE) or a Graduate Diploma in Law (GDL) then follow the law graduate route.

➢ **solicitors** – draw up contracts, assess cases, provide advice and recommend courses of action to clients. First they must take the one-year Legal Practice Course (if they have a law degree) followed by a training contract with a law firm. During your training contract you take a Professional Skills Course (PSC).

Non-law graduates have to study for a Common Professional Examination (CPE) or a Graduate Diploma in Law (GDL) then follow the law graduate route. Another route is to take a Senior Status law degree (two years, full time or three years, part time. This is a non-law graduate conversion course.

➢ **chartered legal executives** – qualified lawyers who work with solicitors and carry out specialist legal work. You can enter training at GCSE level and work your way up (usually via an apprenticeship) but many applicants have higher-level qualifications.

➢ **paralegals** – legal support staff work under the direction of solicitors. There is currently no legal requirement for a paralegal to have legal qualifications, but most law firms want their paralegals to be law or LPC graduates.

➢ **licenced conveyancers** – these are specialised property lawyers, drawing up and transferring leases or deeds for houses etc. You would need to undertake further study to become licensed.

➢ **the police** – the police force is a possibility and as a police officer you would apply your legal knowledge on a day-to-day basis. There are also administrative and specialist support jobs within the police.

Working outside law

A law degree is well respected for many business or management careers. For example, all limited companies must have a company secretary, who has to take on a number of legal responsibilities. You might choose to enter another profession such as accountancy or human resources where knowledge of law could prove useful.

Sources of information

www.barcouncil.org.uk

Chartered Institute of Legal Executives
www.cilexcareers.org.uk

Institute of Paralegals
www.theiop.org

Solicitors Regulation Authority
www.sra.org.uk for list of qualifying law degrees

The Law Society
www.lawsociety.org.uk

www.lawcareers.net

The Beginner's Guide to a Career in Law
www.lawcareers.net/BeginnersGuide/Intro

www.institutelegalsecretaries.com

www.lnat.ac.uk

www.associationofcostslawyers.co.uk

www.skillsforjustice-cp.com

> *'Go to your local magistrates' court and sit in the public gallery. It will give you an instant introduction to law and help you find out if it's for you.'*
> Ahmed, studying a BA in law

MATHEMATICS (including further maths and statistics)

Mathematics is useful in just about every field of human endeavour. It is used in science and exploration, in business and government, in industry and forecasting, and many more areas. Some A level topics follow on from GCSE. You study them in greater depth and then tackle harder and more complicated problems. You will also study new areas, with their own specialised techniques for solving whole new types of problems. Mathematics is a continuous discipline, which means that techniques introduced in one topic must be understood before moving onto the next.

What do you study?

The topics listed give an idea of what could be covered. The exact content of specifications differs according to exam boards. You will need to check with your school or college about the exact options available to you.

The new specifications cover pure mathematics, mechanics and statistics. The assessments have a greater emphasis on modelling, problem-solving and reasoning.

Mathematics can be divided into two areas: pure and applied. Courses consist of about half pure mathematics and half 'applied' topics like mechanics and statistics.

➢ **pure mathematics** – algebra and functions, proof, co-ordinate geometry, trigonometry and vectors, exponentials and logarithms, and powers, differentiation, integration and numerical methods.

Pure mathematics is the foundation for much of the work you do in other areas as well as being the starting point for the study of mathematics at a higher level.

➢ **statistics** – statistical sampling, data presentation and interpretation, probability, statistical distributions, statistical hypothesis testing.

Statistics is used in all areas of science and the social sciences, including psychology, economics, business studies and management. This topic is good preparation for work or further study in any of these areas, especially as many numerate degree courses include modules in statistics.

➢ **mechanics** – quantities and units in mechanics, kinematics, forces and Newton's laws, moments.

Mechanics is important in physics and engineering and in subjects like architecture, physical geography and environmental science. It is the starting point for the study of more advanced topics at a higher level including relativity and elementary particles.

There are some other A/AS levels in mathematics:

➢ **further mathematics** – for more able mathematics students who enjoy the subject and have a real flair for mathematics. In further mathematics courses, the ground covered is both broader and more difficult than the ordinary curriculum. In some cases, it consists of taking more of the optional modules in the ordinary curriculum but studying them in greater depth.

➢ **statistics** – provides a second subject for mathematics. The new specifications have a greater emphasis on the interpretation of statistics. A useful choice for degrees where statistics would be useful such as psychology, sociology or business studies.

Learning mathematics means learning how to use it to solve problems and the only way you can do this is through practice. Classwork involves the teacher explaining new material and then working through examples. You follow this up by tackling new problems, which become more difficult. Some of this work will be done in class, but you should also expect to put in at least five or six hours a week outside lesson time. You do most of your work using pen and paper with the help of calculators (although some modules may be non-calculator) and you will use computers to model systems and try out ideas on a larger scale. As this subject builds continuously on previous work, it can become difficult if you get behind. You must have a very thorough grasp of the fundamentals, so that you can concentrate on the new material.

Use of technology

The use of technology, such as mathematical and statistical graphing tools and spreadsheets, is an essential part of the new maths and statistics A levels.

Calculators used must include the following features: an iterative function and the ability to compute summary statistics and access probabilities from standard statistical distributions. Check with your teachers for advice on which calculators are acceptable.

Maths A levels are examined by written exams.

Subject combinations

Mathematics is used as a tool in many other subjects, from engineering and physics to social sciences and business. Depending on what you want to do, you can combine it with any other subject. If you are thinking of studying mathematics or a related subject at a higher level, you should think about combining it with a science. Physics is a useful preparation for degree courses that include applied mathematics. As well as overlapping with mathematics in some topic areas, physics also uses mathematics more than any other subject, so it can provide valuable practice and support.

Other sciences, and subjects like economics, also involve mathematics and statistics. You might consider further mathematics, as this covers more ground and gives extra depth to your understanding.

A level mathematics and physics are required or preferred for physics and most engineering degrees. If you intend to study A level biology, psychology, geography, sociology, computer science, economics or business studies, you will find that the statistics in A level mathematics or statistics A level will be useful.

Higher education options

A good pass at A level or equivalent is essential if you want to study mathematics successfully at a higher level. If you did not take the right subjects you could consider a foundation year. Some universities offer a foundation year for those not up to undergraduate level standard in mathematics. If you complete this successfully you can transfer to a mathematics or mathematics-related degree.

There are different types of mathematics degrees apart from the BSc. There is a four or five year degree called MMath. Even though the first 'M' stands for 'master', this is an undergraduate degree. The degree is intended for those who want a career in mathematics and/or to undertake postgraduate study in maths. The first two years are the same as the BSc, but the final two years are more demanding. If you enter university on one degree you can transfer to the other and, as the MMath is tougher than the BSc, students who do not maintain a good average grade in their first two years usually transfer to the BSc in their third year. You will also find MSci degrees, which are comparable with masters level study.

Degree-level study

Mathematics at degree level is a natural continuation of A level work in some ways. However, the rate at which you cover new material is much faster and degree-level study is more abstract than at A level and more difficult to relate to common experience. Apart from learning new material, you will develop your problem-solving skills.

The size of the subject means that most mathematics courses are flexible, particularly in the second and third years. You might learn new applications of mathematics such as fluid flow and aerodynamics, alongside developing your understanding of the theoretical underpinning of modern mathematics. In addition to optional modules such as statistics, there may be specialist topics such as quantum mechanics, mathematical modelling, cryptography and topology. Some courses offer a mathematics-related module such as business, computing or accounting.

There are also many specialist courses that allow you to concentrate on one area from the start. These include courses in the main areas of the subject, like pure mathematics, applied mathematics and discrete mathematics. Other courses concentrate on particular application areas like engineering mathematics or financial mathematics, mathematical physics and mathematics education (which leads to a teaching qualification in addition to a degree). Some courses offer a year abroad spent studying at another university and some offer industrial placements.

Degree subject combinations

You may want to combine mathematics with a completely different subject to provide variety, but there are also plenty of opportunities to take combined courses in which mathematics and the other subject support and complement each other. Such subjects include physics (there are also specialist mathematical physics courses), operational research and statistics. There is also a specialist MORSE BSc which combines mathematics, operations research, statistics and economics.

Other higher education qualifications

There are foundation degrees in education and training for maths and numeracy specialist learning assistants in secondary schools (mathematics and education) and in related subjects like accounting, business, engineering and IT. There is an HND in mathematics and computing, again consider related areas such as business, accountancy, engineering and IT.

Relevance to other subjects?

Mathematics A level is accepted as a good entry qualification for almost any other subject at degree level. It is needed for most physics and engineering courses and is strongly recommended or compulsory for many chemistry courses. Although not always a requirement for courses in biological sciences, it can be very useful, especially for the statistical part of the degree. Statistics is useful for courses in psychology, geography, sociology, business studies and economics, and is often a requirement for economics and computer science degrees.

A level mathematics can be used as an alternative to A level physics for entry to some courses. For example, the A level requirements for medicine, dentistry and veterinary science are usually for mathematics or physics in addition to chemistry (usually compulsory) and biology (usually recommended).

Important advice

In order to succeed in mathematics you must work consistently over a long period. You get into a regular routine of work that will allow you to build up your skills and knowledge. If you are considering a gap year before taking a mathematics degree it is important to check with universities to see how they view it. Some universities feel that you lose continuity in your studies. If you decide to take a gap year, it would be wise to keep up your mathematics during your time out and revise it just before starting your course.

Future careers

After A levels

An A level in mathematics is in great demand by employers. Even when a job does not require specific mathematical knowledge, employers find that the discipline learned through studying mathematics helps you think clearly and logically. You will find people with A level mathematics working in areas that make obvious use of mathematical skills, such as accountancy, banks and financial services, but you are equally likely to find them working as a retail manager in a shop or department store, or as a website or computer games designer. Look at Higher and Degree Apprenticeships that may be available to you after A levels. They are currently available in maths-related areas such as accounting, banking, business admin, insurance, IT, life and chemical sciences, management, audit, tax, management consulting, management accounting, retail management and supply chain management.

After a degree

Working in mathematics

There are many areas where you can use the expertise developed during your degree. These include the following:

➤ **business, finance and accountancy** – this is the single largest career area for graduates in mathematics and statistics. Accountancy will require further training and there are opportunities in private practice, local and central government and business. Banks and other financial services companies like to recruit mathematics and statistics graduates to their management training schemes

➢   **IT** – some graduates go into mathematical computing, but the majority go into more general areas such as programming, systems analysis or consultancy

➢   **actuarial work** – graduates start as trainees and take professional exams

➢   **statistician** – collecting, analysing and interpreting data. Opportunities in government departments, business, finance and research

➢   **operational research/management science** – use advanced analytical methods to solve problems in business, industry and government. A competitive area and postgraduate qualifications often required

➢   **management** – mathematical techniques are used as management tools for solving a variety of complex problems in production, distribution, marketing and financial investment

➢   **technology** – industries such as aerospace, renewable energy and telecommunications employ mathematics graduates for analysing data and working on the design of products or industrial control systems

➢   **education** – there is a demand for qualified mathematics teachers so you may be eligible for financial help with your training

➢   **research** – nearly 23% of mathematics graduates go on to further study or research in mathematics. However, the number finally making a career in research is very much smaller. Some large companies and government organisations also employ research mathematicians, but again the numbers are small compared to the number of graduates.

Working outside mathematics

As most jobs involve some use of numerical or financial data, mathematics graduates are well placed in the job market, provided that they can bring other skills like communication, team working and management potential. Many employers are more interested in a mathematician's ability to analyse and solve problems than any specific mathematical training. Employers include local government, the Civil Service and all areas of industry and business.

Sources of information

www.psiweb.org

Institute of Mathematics and its Applications
www.ima.org.uk

Royal Statistical Society
www.rss.org.uk

www.mathscareers.org.uk

The Operational Research Society
www.theorsociety.com

'The maths department offers lots of extra help, which has really helped my confidence; there are weekly 'maths surgeries' where postgrads are available to help you, a scheme where first years can buddy up with a mentor and tutors who are very supportive.'
Stewart, first year BSc maths

MEDIA STUDIES

Media reflects and influences all aspects of our society. It has developed to the point where anybody can produce their own media products or contribute to the production of media. In media studies you will gain an understanding of all types of media; film, music, newspapers, radio, magazines, games and social media such as Facebook, blogs, Instagram and Twitter. You will develop an understanding of media products and how they are researched, produced, distributed and 'consumed'. You will learn theory and critical analysis as well as some of the practical and technical skills involved in producing media products. You will also consider the cultural, social and political implications of media today. For example, why do more people vote on talent shows that vote in national elections? How do mobile phones and Twitter influence the news media? How about online petitions?

What do you study?

The topics listed give an idea of what could be covered. The exact content of specifications differs according to exam boards. You will need to check with your school or college about the exact options available to you.

You will study all forms of media including television, film, radio, newspapers, magazines, advertising and marketing, online, social and participatory media, video games and music video. The range of products you study will be global and will include media produced before 1950, media produced for a non-English speaking audience, media produced outside the commercial mainstream and media that is targeting, or produced by, a minority group.

➤ **Media language** – how the media, through their forms, codes, conventions and techniques, communicate meanings.

➤ **Representation** – how media forms portray events, issues, individuals and social groups.

➤ **Media institutions** – how the media industries' processes of production, distribution and circulation affect media forms and platforms; patterns of ownership and control including conglomerate ownership, vertical integration and diversification; economic factors, including commercial and not-for-profit public funding; how media organisations maintain, including through marketing, varieties of audiences nationally and globally; the regulatory framework of media in the UK; the impact of 'new' digital technologies on media regulation including the role of individual producers.

➤ **Audiences** – how the media forms target, reach and address audiences, how audiences interpret and respond to them and how audiences can become producers themselves; how audiences are grouped and categorised by media industries including by age, gender and social class as well as by lifestyle and taste; how media producers target, attract, reach, address and potentially construct audiences; how media institutions target audiences through the content and appeal of media products and through the ways in which they are marketed, distributed and circulated ; the interrelationship between media technologies and patterns of consumption and response; how audiences interpret the media, including how they may interpret the same media in different ways; how audiences interact with the media and can be actively involved in media production.

➢ **Cultural, historical and theoretical** – the cultural, social and historical significance of media products, the theoretical frameworks underlying the study of media as well at the theoretical perspectives associated with them.

➢ **Critical analysis** – looking critically at quality, form and structure and engaging in interpretation and in-depth critical analysis, so you develop a detailed understanding of how the media communicate meanings and how audiences respond; you also look at the emerging, future developments of the media .

➢ **Practical techniques** – learning the technical skills to create media products and creating your own. 30% of the marks are through non-exam assessment and you will create media products to a set brief.

A GCSE in media studies is not required for this course but you would be expected to be familiar with a wide range of media products.

Practical classes involve learning how to research and create a media product. You might make a trailer for a TV soap, documentary or thriller, an advertisement, a short interview or news round-up for a radio broadcast, a design for a new women's magazine or create a website. When you are presenting results of any research or project you will use appropriate technologies such as a PowerPoint presentation, a blog, a podcast or a DVD or memory stick with 'extras'.

Subject combinations
Media studies complements many other A levels because it covers such a wide range of subjects. If you are thinking of studying media at a higher level, then English, politics, sociology and psychology could prove useful. For practical courses in media production, it may be an advantage to have an art and design A level, or even maths and sciences for the more technical courses.

Higher education options

An A level in media studies is not required in order to study the subject at a higher level.

Degree-level study

Courses in media studies vary greatly. You will find some focus on culture and media in society and others are more practical. Many institutions offer practical courses in subjects such as digital media and media production (some media production courses have specialisms such as film and radio). Note that some courses might ask for either an Art Foundation course and/or a portfolio of your work for entry. There are also sandwich courses available with a placement in industry or the opportunity to study abroad.

You will also find more specialist courses such as digital marketing, internet applications, journalism or sports journalism. If you don't want to specialise at first degree level there are opportunities for postgraduate study in media specialisms such as journalism or media production.

Degree subject combinations

The subjects most widely available in combination with media studies are English, history and politics. If you want to get a job in the media, which is competitive, it would be a good idea to combine media studies with a subject that might help you to get a start in your career, such as business studies, politics, modern languages or sciences.

Other higher education qualifications

There are foundation degrees available in media, media practice and media production. You will also find lots of related courses such as, broadcast media, creative media production (games design), interactive media, media skills, visual media production and wildlife education and media.

Media studies can be taken at HND or HNC level and courses include creative media production, games design for industry and media and communication.

Relevance to other subjects?

Media studies A level helps you to develop useful skills relevant to a number of other subjects. Your ability to analyse and criticise visual, written and audio information in relation to cultural, political and social factors would help with subjects such as English, history of art, drama and theatre studies, design courses, archaeology, philosophy and modern languages. Your understanding of the political and social influences at work in the media would also help you in the study of most social science courses, such as sociology, psychology, politics or history.

Important advice

There are many media courses on offer. If you are even remotely considering a career in the media, you should make sure that the course you choose offers the balance that you want between practical and theoretical work. It is a good idea to check out the range of practical facilities offered, such as recording equipment and editing facilities. Make sure you research the destinations of graduates from your chosen courses and check what links they have with employers.

Don't forget that if you are planning a career in the media you should be building up experience now, even if it is on the school website or hospital radio. Also networking is key to a media career so start building up your networks now.

Future careers

After A levels

Media studies is useful in many areas of work, particularly if they involve communication and up-to-date media knowledge. The media industries are difficult to get into, so you may need further qualifications and experience. However there are some apprenticeships available which could prove a very useful entry into media. Creative Skillset run apprenticeships in creative and digital media and there are also broadcast production and technology Higher Apprenticeships. You could also consider business and administration apprenticeships as a way of getting into media companies.

After a degree

Working in the media

It is hard for media studies graduates to get started in media. Any contacts made during your degree may eventually become useful to you so it is important to keep networking and get as much relevant work experience as you can, to build up your CV/portfolio. Organisations such as the BBC offer work experience placements and you may be able to arrange your own work placement or internship. If you are hoping to enter TV or film production, you should be prepared to get further training, or to start in a junior position. You may have to arrange and finance extra training yourself to get you the right skills and knowledge.

Don't forget that the media industry is a very broad one and covers not only the obvious jobs in journalism, interactive media, film and TV. There are also opportunities in animation, computer games, advertising, facilities (specialist technical services to film and TV), photo imaging and publishing.

Here are some examples of popular jobs in the media:

➤ **media planners** – they identify which media platforms would best advertise a client's brand or product. They work within advertising agencies or media planning and buying agencies. They enable their clients to maximise the impact of their advertising campaigns through the use of a range of media

➤ **multimedia specialists** – combines creative and technical skills to design products for many different users. These might be computer animations, audio, video and graphic image files for multimedia applications including computer games. They also plan, produce and maintain web sites and web applications using web programming, scripting, authoring, content management and file transfer software

➤ **journalists** – in radio, TV, newspapers, magazines, blogs or digital/social media

➤ **production/broadcasting assistants** – in film and television they help to run the producers' and directors' offices, involved in programmes from planning to post- production

➤ **technicians** – technical jobs arranging lighting or sound in studios or on location for outside broadcasts

➤ **researchers** – they work mainly on factual research for programmes, including films and documentaries.

Working outside the media

There are many career areas where you could make use of your knowledge and skills. Your understanding of how images are created and the effect that they have on consumers would be useful in public relations. Marketing may also be a good choice, as it involves identifying the kind of product that the public would like to buy, and managing the packaging, advertising and selling of that product. You will have developed good communication and teamwork skills, which could be applied to many areas of business.

Sources of information

www.bbc.co.uk/careers

www.bfi.org.uk

www.bima.co.uk

www.creativeskillset.org/careers

www.itvjobs.com

'Applying for media jobs starts off with lots of rejections, but you only need one yes.'
Phillip, aged 25, working in PR after a journalism degree

MODERN FOREIGN LANGUAGES

'If you talk to a man in a language he understands, that goes to his head. If you talk to him in his own language, that goes to his heart.'
Nelson Mandela

Languages are all around us; they are used in so many situations whether at work, on holiday or just in daily life – we live in a multilingual global society.

Neglecting languages in business means ignoring significant potential markets. Apart from the business aspect, language study not only gives you language and communication skills, but also a way of understanding a society and its culture. The most-widely used languages on the internet are English, Chinese, Spanish, Arabic, then Portuguese, Japanese, Russian, Malay, French and German. The official languages of the United Nations are Arabic, Chinese, English, French, Russian and Spanish.

The new language specifications are designed to help students develop and deepen their awareness and understanding of the language, as well as of their cultural, literary and social knowledge about the communities and countries where the languages are spoken, through the study of the language in its cultural, literary and social context.

A range of modern foreign languages is available at A level, including French, German, Spanish, Italian, Chinese, Japanese and Russian.

You are encouraged to learn languages within the context of the culture, society and way of life of the countries where they are spoken, including current issues affecting the country. You might also focus on how the language is used in business; the top business languages required by UK employers are currently Chinese, German, French, Arabic, Spanish, Portuguese and Russian.

While many people focus on the up and coming economies around the world, you shouldn't ignore the benefit of learning core European languages; besides being spoken in Europe, they all have a global reach, including South America and Africa.

➢ **French** is the most popular choice. France is one of our nearest neighbours and for a country so close, French culture, philosophy, literature are quite different from our own. Studying French brings you into close contact with the country's traditions and gives you direct access to its rich literary and artistic traditions. Becoming fluent in French you won't just be able to converse with professionals in France, but also in parts of Canada, African countries such as Cameroon or Senegal, and Switzerland.

➤ **Germany** is a centre for finance and manufacturing in Europe, so many businesses in the UK and throughout the world have established trade links in the country German has many similarities to English, and some English learners find it easier to pronounce than French. One major difference between German and either English or French is that German grammar makes more use of 'inflection' – changes of word ending to indicate a change in meaning (as in English singular and plural, for example). This means that getting started can seem more difficult than with a language like French, but once you get past this, you can progress at a similar rate. Once you have the basics, German can provide you with an understanding of a culture with a complex political history and a rich literary, musical and dramatic tradition. It is also spoken in Austria, Switzerland, Namibia and by some Eastern Europeans.

➤ **Spanish** is a language that you may find quite easy, especially if you have already studied French (although it gets more difficult later). It is the world's second most widely spoken language (after Chinese) and has the advantage of opening up the language and literature of most of Latin America as well as Spain. Spanish is an important language in the USA as well. The Spanish language has travelled throughout the world, most notably in South and Central America where it is the predominant language.

➤ **Chinese (Mandarin)** is one of the fastest growing languages in the world. With over a billion speakers, in China and other nations, it is quickly becoming one of the most popular second languages – particularly amongst professionals. More businesses are now expanding into China or using suppliers and manufacturers within the country, which means that there are more opportunities for multi-lingual employees.

➤ **Italian**, like Spanish, will be easier for you to learn if you have already started French. It is perhaps less likely than French, Spanish or German to be useful to you in your career but is still an important business and cultural language.

➤ **Russian** is another language that has experienced huge growth in recent years, closely mirroring the increased trade with businesses in Russia, Kazakhstan and other surrounding nations. As demand for Russian speaking experts increases, so too does the value placed on developing fluent language skills. Companies from around the world are flocking to former Soviet states to establish business links and broker deals, adding further value to mastering the Russian language. Russian is more difficult than the other frequently taught languages, not least because it has a different alphabet. However, most learners soon master this and find it to be a rewarding language to learn.

What do you study?

The topics listed give an idea of what could be covered. The exact content of specifications differs according to exam boards. You will need to check with your school or college about the exact options available to you.

Learning a language can be broken down into four skills – writing, reading, speaking and listening (understanding the spoken language).

➢ **Writing** – the ability to communicate in the written language using the appropriate style and form for the communication required. This may involve tasks such as writing a reply to a formal or informal letter, job applications or writing a promotional leaflet. You will have to express your ideas in the form of essays and short-answer questions on a wide range of topics including current issues, the arts, education or literature, written in your chosen language.

➢ **Reading** – you will be encouraged to read texts regularly in your chosen language. Some of these may be literary texts in the form of plays, poetry, prose or film. You will read newspapers and magazines in the chosen language to develop your vocabulary and comprehension. You will be tested, mainly in the chosen language, with comprehension questions of various types. Some demand short answers or are multiple-choice questions, but others require more extensive writing. One purpose of this is to demonstrate your understanding of what you read; in the case of literary work, your appreciation is assessed as well as your understanding.

➢ **Speaking** – the ability to express yourself clearly and correctly through spoken language. You will be encouraged to develop a wide vocabulary and practise speaking in the language as often as possible in order to develop a comfortable and grammatically accurate style. All specifications require an oral exam, and you will be given plenty of practice at taking part in general conversation as well as speaking on specific topics.

30% of the marks for the new A level are gained through non-exam assessment, which will test your spoken skills through conversation, debates and presentations.

➢ **Listening** – gaining skills in listening and understanding the language, including its informal use by native speakers in the different countries and communities where it may be spoken. This is done using a variety of different media such as radio, TV, cinema and the web. While working on all these skills you learn about the society, culture, education, institutions and economy of the country or countries where the language is spoken. The exams will effectively test your knowledge of these issues as well as your command of the language.

A good pass at GCSE in the language is usually required in order to take the A level language.

You will work individually and in groups with written texts from newspapers and magazines and multimedia recordings. You will watch recorded programmes and films and then discuss them, working on the vocabulary that you learn and the grammatical points that they illustrate. Outside class, there is a good deal of time spent committing things to memory – especially vocabulary. There may be the opportunity to go on a trip to the relevant country or you may be able to go on an exchange programme and live in the country for a while.

Subject combinations

If you are thinking of specialising in modern foreign languages at degree level, you may prefer to make an early start by studying two languages for A level (although you can nearly always start a second language as a beginner at degree level). If you take two languages, you should find that the skills and knowledge relating to the workings of one language will help you with the other. This is also the case if you combine a modern foreign language with an A level in classical/ancient Greek or Latin. You could combine a language with many other subjects including business, computer science and sciences.

Higher education options

There are opportunities to study language degrees without having an A level in the language and you will learn the subject from scratch (also known as ab initio). However, for French degrees virtually all institutions require A level French (a few will accept an A level in another language). The same applies to a lesser extent to German and Spanish. For other languages universities will expect students to be beginners. However, a language A level, even in a different language, will help as it proves you have language learning skills and experience.

Degree-level study

Language study at degree level varies between courses. At some, you would find a big difference from your A level studies as you would spend a large proportion of your time studying literature. At others, the focus remains on practical language use and the study of contemporary society. There are modern languages degrees where you might study two or even three languages.

A popular option is to build on your existing skills and knowledge by continuing with your A level language and starting a new one alongside it. At some institutions you can choose from a wide range of languages that may not have been available to you at A level, such as Scandinavian languages, Portuguese, Arabic, Chinese, Japanese or African languages.

Another option is a regional studies course, which allows you to study one or two modern languages alongside the economic, political, social, legal and cultural climates of that country or region. European studies is the most widely offered but there are also emerging degrees in Asia Pacific studies and Latin American/Hispanic studies. It is assumed that you already have a strong grasp of your major chosen language, unless it wasn't available to you at A level. There a few universities who offer a foundation year if you have the aptitude but not the right qualifications for entry.

Don't forget that there are many business degrees with an international focus that also offer the opportunity to continue your language studies or learn a new language from scratch.

On nearly all language degrees you will spend some time abroad. This is usually the third of your four years. There are many opportunities available and you might study, teach or undertake a work placement.

Degree subject combinations

Modern foreign languages can be usefully combined with a wide range of other subjects. With increasing economic, political and cultural contacts throughout the world, a carefully chosen combination can increase your employment options. Economics, business studies, engineering, marketing, politics, a science subject or law could be particularly appropriate. Combined subject degrees are available almost everywhere. Some institutions have created specialist 'European' or 'international' degrees in subjects such as engineering, sciences and law (where you may study French or German law and language, or EU law, as well as English law). In these, your language study is more likely to be integrated with your study of the other subject than it is in a standard two-subject degree course. You will find specialised combined degrees to cater for emerging markets; Chinese, for example, can be combined with finance, business or law.

Other higher education qualifications

There are no foundation degrees in modern foreign languages but some HNDs and HNCs in tourism management offer options in modern foreign languages.

Chartered Institute of Linguists qualifications

The Chartered Institute of Linguists runs qualifications in translating and interpreting. These can be studied full or part time and at different levels of language proficiency.

Relevance to other subjects?

Even if you decide not to study modern foreign languages by themselves at a higher level, you will find your study valuable. A knowledge of a modern foreign language at A level would help in the study of English, especially English language, history, politics and philosophy. If you are interested not just in one or two languages but language in general, you might consider a degree in linguistics, in which you study the development of human language: its structures, history and use. Since linguistics study must be backed up with examples from particular languages, knowledge of a modern foreign language will be very useful to you; you can also combine language study with linguistics.

Important advice

No matter how much classroom work you do, there is no substitute for experiencing a language first hand. Try to visit a country where your chosen language is spoken and spend time listening to it and speaking it, as well as absorbing the country's culture. It's easy to listen to the radio on the internet and this can only help you with your studies. Nearly all universities have language centres, so even if you decide not to study your languages as part of a degree, you are likely to have the opportunity to continue your studies part time at a university language centre.

Future careers

After A levels

You will find the level of language that you achieve with A level study is an advantage when you apply for practically any sort of job, especially with companies trading internationally. There are some opportunities to go straight from A levels into a job where your language skills will be used every day, such as working for an airline as cabin crew or ground staff, or within the travel industry, perhaps as a rep for a tour company at home or abroad. There are Higher Apprenticeships in hospitality management, business and logistics where languages might be put to good use working for international companies.

After a degree

Working in modern foreign languages

Language-based careers are a popular choice for language graduates. You normally have to undertake further specialist training if you wish to become a professional linguist. There are three traditional language-based career roles – interpreters, translators or teachers. These can be combined in a number of careers:

➢ **interpreters** – they translate the spoken language, normally into their own mother tongue. Interpreters provide an essential link between businesses or governments during negotiations or they may work translating for foreign nationals abroad. The work may be face-to-face or over the telephone. This kind of work requires further training and fluency in languages, preferably including a degree in an unusual language.

➢ **translators** – they work with the written language and the normal practice is to translate into the native language from the second language, not vice versa. They are often self-employed and work mainly for businesses. Some translators group together to form agencies offering translation in a wide range of languages.

➢ **teachers** – language teachers are always in demand so the more subjects or languages you are able to teach, the more valuable you are likely to be.

➢ **travel and tourism** – there are many opportunities here, whether you are working in the UK or abroad, ranging from tour guide to management positions. You could be using your languages on a daily basis and your knowledge of the country and culture to help you communicate effectively.

Here are some examples of jobs where languages will be useful:

➢ **computer games translator** – translating computer games into other languages

➢ **website translator** – more and more websites are multi-lingual or need to have a version for different language speakers

➢ **football analyst** – watching and analysing the latest European football matches and producing reports on the failures and successes of the team. These are passed on to traders to aid investors in betting more successfully

➢ **international relocation manager** – working for large international companies to help staff relocate to new countries. You organise housing, schools for their children and removals

➢ **group tour organiser** – organising tours for musical groups like orchestras or theatre companies; organising and booking venues, hotels and transport

➢ **journalist** – using your language skills to research and write articles for magazines

➢ **press conference assistant** – interpreting for foreign language speakers at press conferences. Think of all the football players and managers who may need this service

➢ **recruitment consultant** – recruiting globally in a wide range of employment sectors.

You will find languages skills in demand in most areas of work. Examples of areas using languages skills include: IT, creative and media, national and local government, hospitably and tourism, manufacturing, construction, logistics, property management, engineering, import and export, finance and business.

Working outside modern foreign languages

Graduate linguists are good candidates for most jobs open to graduates in any subject as they are flexible thinkers, imaginative and creative. They also have a unique understanding and appreciation of other cultures. Many find that they do not use their languages at the start of their career – for example, they may be engaged in general management training. If they maintain their language skills there could be opportunities to use them later on.

Sources of information

Chartered Institute of Linguists
www.ciol.org.uk

www.studyinglanguages.ac.uk/

www.whystudylanguages.ac.uk

www.thirdyearabroad.com

https://getintoteaching.education.gov.uk/explore-my-options/teach-languages

> *'My favourite part of this degree has always been the language itself. Going from year to year, including my time spent abroad, the language lectures become increasingly more challenging, which has shown me just how far I have come with my learning.'*
> Mike, French undergraduate

MUSIC

If you are a keen musician, this course gives you the chance to develop your musical abilities and acquire an in-depth knowledge and understanding of musical elements, musical contexts and musical language. You will also learn the skills to appraise a piece of music. You will be able to demonstrate your skills in musical performance and study musical theory, composition and arranging. Some specifications allow you to study world music, folk music, jazz, music for media and gaming, theatre music and contemporary electronic/minimalist music in addition to the classical music of Western Europe. Students learn to work together well in addition to developing performing, composing and critical or analytical skills. The course develops versatility, creative ability and good communication skills.

What do you study?

Music A level specifications are broadly alike, but have different options within them. Most allow you to choose where you want to place the emphasis of your own studies. You study a number of the following, depending on the course options you choose. Some offer different pathways for composers and performers. Some include music technology although this is also available as a separate A level.

➢ **Appraising** – learning how to appraise, develop and demonstrate an in-depth knowledge and understanding of musical elements, musical contexts and musical language. This will involve the study of pieces of music from different periods and genres, right up to the present day. This will involve written work.

Music genres and periods (depending on the exam board) include:
- **Western classical music 1650–1910**: a wide range of composers and genres such as Barowue, Mozart, Haydn, and Beethoven; the piano music of Chopin, Brahms and Grieg
- **Pop music**: Stevie Wonder, Joni Mitchell, Muse, Beyoncé, Daft Punk, Labrinth
- **Music for media**: that is music composed for film, television and gaming from 1958 to the present. Composers include Bernard Herrmann, Hans Zimmer, Michael Giacchino, Thomas Newman, Nobuo Uematsu
- **Music for theatre**: from 1930 to the present: Kurt Weill, Richard Rodgers, Stephen Sondheim, Claude-Michel Schönberg, Jason Robert Brown
- **Jazz**: musicians such as Louis Armstrong, Duke Ellington, Charlie Parker, Miles Davis, Pat Metheny, Gwilym Simcock
- **Contemporary traditional music**: defined as music influenced by traditional musical features fused with contemporary elements and styles. Astor Piazzolla,Toumani Diabaté, Anoushka Shankar, Mariza, Bellowhead

- **Art music since 1910**: this is music since 1910 that comprises modern, contemporary classical, electronic art, experimental and minimalist music as well as other forms. Dmitri Shostakovich, Olivier Messiaen, Steve Reich, James MacMillan.

You might also study blues, swing and big band, religious music and innovations in music from 1900 to the present day.

➢ **Performing** – preparing a recital lasting between 5 and 16 minutes (depending on the exam board). This might be a solo performance or as part of an ensemble or a music production.

➢ **Composing** – learning the techniques of musical composition. This could be learning about choral harmonisations in the style of J.S. Bach, keyboard accompaniment in the early Romantic style, minimalism or contemporary developments such as the popular song, folk, club dance, hip-hop, music theatre and world music. As well as composing, you will carry out exercises in arrangement – the preparation of a given piece of music for a particular instrument or group of instruments. You may be required to write a commentary or notes on your work and how you created it. Some exam boards require composition as part of a formal examination and you might have to write a composition to a brief as well as having the opportunity to write your own work.

Performance and composition form 60% of the A level assessment, which could be a combination of 25% performance and 35% composition, or 35% performing and 25% composing, depending on the exam board. 40% is by written examination.

A good grade (B or above or grade 5/6 or better with the new, revised GCSE) in GCSE music may be required before you can study the A level. Sometimes grade 5 musical theory is accepted in place of the GCSE. You will be expected to play a musical instrument to a certain standard, which can vary between Associated Board of the Royal Schools of Music grade 4 and 6, depending on your school or college.

In some ways, music is like a language. You have to learn how it is put together (techniques such as harmony and types of musical form) and how it conveys feelings, mental images and moods. As with learning a language, improvement comes largely from exposure and lots of practice. Much of your time will be spent listening to music, discussing and analysing what you have heard and developing your ability to listen actively. Your ability to analyse different pieces of music depends on your experience of a wide variety of different types of music, so as well as your set work you should go to as many live music events as possible. If your course involves performance, you will have to spend quite a lot of time practising your instrument or instruments.

Subject combinations

Music can be combined with any other A level. If you are thinking of studying music in higher education, especially if you are thinking of a singing career, languages are very useful. If you are considering a course in music technology or electronic music, then mathematics, physics or computer science will be useful.

Higher education options

A good pass in A level music is usually required in order to be able to study it at a higher level. For many courses you have to pass a performance test and/or offer a pass at a high level (usually grade 8) in the Associated Board of the Royal Schools of Music graded examinations.

Degree-level study

Depending on your interests you can take a music degree course at university, where you will be studying alongside students in other disciplines, or at a music college (conservatoire), which is geared more towards performance.

Music courses usually lead to either a BA (Bachelor of Arts) or BMus (Bachelor of Music) degree. The BMus is much the same as a BA but when an institution offers both a BA and a BMus, the BA is typically broader in scope while the BMus concentrates more on composition, history or performance. You should check the course details carefully. You would probably spend the first two years of a music degree course developing the skills and knowledge that you gained at A level, your understanding of music theory and history, and your performance skills. In the final year, you have the chance to concentrate on the aspects of music that you find the most interesting.

Your specialised options might include the study of a particular period of musical history; works written for choirs, the piano, stringed instruments or another family of instruments; non-classical music, such as jazz or rock; or the use of computers in music composition. Some institutions also offer the chance to spend part of your time studying abroad in a conservatoire or university.

There are also degrees concentrating on specialist areas like new music, community music, popular music, song writing and music production and musical theatre.

Conservatoires: as mentioned earlier, these offer more performance-based degrees and have a separate application and selection process.

- Birmingham Conservatoire
- Leeds College of Music
- Royal Academy of Music
- Royal College of Music
- Royal Conservatoire of Scotland
- Royal Northern College of Music
- Royal Welsh College of Music and Drama
- Trinity Laban Conservatoire of Music and Dance.

The Guildhall School of Music and Drama does not recruit through the UCAS Conservatoires system. Applicants should apply direct.

You can research courses on the UCAS Conservatoires website, www.ucas.com/ucas/conservatoires

Degree subject combinations

University-based courses give you the opportunity to study music as part of a combined degree scheme or modular course, with a wide range of other subjects. You might consider a performing arts or creative arts course, in which you can usually study a combination of drama, music and visual art. Alternatively, you can combine music with any other subject including business, maths, English, history, sciences or modern languages. There are various options and specialisms in music education if you wish to teach.

Other higher education qualifications

There are many foundation degrees in music including music production, popular music, sound and music technology, creative music production and business and music technology.

HNDs and HNCs are available in music, music performance, music (contemporary and jazz performance), DJ and electronic music production, music production, music - venue performance and studio skills, urban and electronic music, music performance and technology and live sounds and events.

Relevance to other subjects?

An A level in music doesn't have to lead to a music course at a conservatoire or university. Many people find that their musical knowledge and understanding of the 'language' of music is extremely useful in subjects such as drama, modern foreign languages, philosophy, linguistics and communication studies.

Important advice

The selection procedure for a higher level course in music can be very tough. You may be required to reach a performance level equivalent to the grade 8 practical music examination. If you do not have this, you might be asked to submit a certified audio or video recording of your performance for review, as evidence of equivalence. In addition to a general interview, you may be asked to perform a piece of music and to take a listening test and a sight-reading test, or something similar. Find out whether you are likely to have to attend a practical audition. The UCAS Conservatoires website has some useful information on auditions. Remember you are likely to have to pay an audition fee in addition to your application fee.

Future careers

After A levels

An A level in music may not lead directly to a music career but it can give you an advantage in careers where musical knowledge would be useful. Provided you don't mind starting at the bottom and doing junior jobs like running errands and making the tea, you might find work in the recording industry, for a music magazine or website, or at a radio station. There may also be apprenticeships in the music business. A level music can be used as a general qualification for entry to careers in many businesses or organisations.

After a degree

Working in music

Many careers relating to music involve additional training and experience before they can really take off properly. These include the following:

➤ **performing** – as a soloist, part of a small ensemble or larger orchestra, or as a piano accompanist for other performers. This sort of work requires a very high standard, continual practice and often unsocial working hours. There is also a good deal of competition and you will have to take whatever work you can get. If you have the relevant experience and ability, you may be able to supplement your performing income with private or school teaching.

➢ **media** – there is an increasing demand for music of all types for broadcasting on radio, TV and the internet, and therefore a number of career opportunities in the areas of presenting, writing (for computer games, for example) and in music technology generally.

➢ **teaching** – including private tuition to individual students, as well as class teaching in schools. For teaching in state schools, you will need a recognised teaching qualification. You may also gain work as a peripatetic teacher, moving round to different schools to give lessons.

➢ **music technician** – as a technician rather than a performer, you might be responsible for sound quality or technical equipment either in the recording studio or as part of a team at a performance.

➢ **music business management** – organising performances, contracts, rehearsals and publicity on behalf of musicians. You might work for a large symphony orchestra, jazz band or pop band.

➢ **composing** – not many people earn a living as a composer, and they usually build up their careers gradually. They might work on commissions awarded by advertisers or television and radio producers, often spending weeks working painstakingly on pieces lasting only 15 seconds.

➢ **music therapy** – working with adults and children with injuries or disabilities, making use of both the physical skills and emotional dimension of music to develop or restore people's abilities. You would need a further qualification for this.

Working outside music

Because of the option to teach, quite a high proportion of music graduates do work professionally in music after they graduate. Some use their practical skills and knowledge in other careers. Some of these will have a connection with music, including arts administration, broadcast engineer, sound engineer, libraries and publishing. Others take further training and enter completely different careers.

Sources of information

British Association for Music Therapy
www.bamt.org

Incorporated Society of Musicians
www.ism.org

http://getintomusic.org/

http://www.careersinmusic.co.uk/

> *'I liked the fact that many of my lecturers and tutors were still playing and composing. It was a privilege to be taught by them.'*
> Paula, BMus graduate

MUSIC TECHNOLOGY

Every piece of music you listen to has been arranged, recorded, mixed and produced by someone. Music technology at A level is for students who want to learn about recording, mixing, arranging and producing music. It teaches you how to use current and developing technology creatively to arrange and compose music as well as developing your musical skills and learning skills for music production.

What do you study?

The topics listed give an idea of what could be covered. The exact content of specifications differs according to exam boards. You will need to check with your school or college about the exact options available to you.

➢ **Recording and production techniques** – learning the skills required to produce and record musical performances in a range of styles. You will learn the various methods and techniques of doing this including software and hardware, capture of sound, sequencing and MIDI/OSC, audio editing, EQ, dynamic processing, effects, balance and blend, stereo, synthesis, sampling, automation, pitch and rhythm correction/manipulation and mastering.

➢ **Principles of sound and audio technology** – different factors involved starting with acoustics and sound waves and then looking at hardware such as speakers, leads, digital and analogue records and sound levels. You will also learn technical numeracy, for example displaying graphic information, interpreting graphs making calculations to describe sound waves including waveforms, frequency, phase and amplitude.

➢ **Development of recording and production technology** – looking at how the technology has developed from direct to tape and mono recording in the 1950s right up to digital recording and sequencing, and digital audio workstations used in the present day. You look at how this different technology has been used to create and shape sound, including electric and electronic instruments, multi-track recording and equipment used, samplers and synthesisers.

➢ **The impact of music technology** – on creative processes in the studio and in the wider context of music technology and how it has influenced trends in music e.g. computer games, popular music, film score, soundscapes in art installations, sound effects for film.

➢ **Ethical and legal** – understanding ethical and legal implications of copyright in relation to composing, performing and recording and the role of intellectual property within the music industry.

> **Arranging and production skills** – developing the ability to use music production tools and techniques to capture sounds with accuracy and control, manipulating existing sounds and music with technical control and style, effectively using processing techniques to produce a balanced final mix, developing competence as a music producer and sound engineer by producing recordings and technology-based compositions.

> **Composition** – you will use a combination of technical and musical skills to apply musical elements and language e.g. structure, timbre, texture, tempo and rhythm, melody, harmony and tonality, and dynamics, to develop imaginative compositions within the context of music technology, and create new sounds and music. You will make informed decisions about equipment by analysing and interpreting a range of data, graphical representations and diagrams relating to frequency response, microphone polar patterns and dynamic response.

> **Listening and analysing critically** – you develop the ability to analyse the musical, technical, production and stylistic features of music and consider the impact of technology on music. You will use these listening skills to identify and evaluate music technology elements in unfamiliar works and to refine recordings and technology-based compositions

The A level will give you the skills to respond creatively to a brief, and develop effectiveness as a music producer, sound engineer and creative artist by producing recordings and technology-based compositions.

40% of the A level marks are gained through non-exam assessments. You will demonstrate use of music technology to create, edit and structure sounds to develop a technology-based composition, as well as use music technology to capture, edit and produce recordings.

GCSE music may be a requirement for this course unless you have previous experience. No experience in music technology is required but you may be asked to play a musical instrument to a certain level for entry to the course.

Subject combinations

If you wish to study music technology at a higher level, you should select other A levels from mathematics, physics, computer science, electronics or music depending on the content and requirements of the course. Some courses will require music A level in addition to music technology, or require you to reach a certain standard of performance (which could include an audition).

Higher education options

Degree-level study

Music technology is a popular area of study and attracts students from both musical and technical backgrounds who want to learn about both cutting-edge technical and creative developments in the field. There is a variety of degrees available with varying titles including music technology, creative music technology, digital music and sound arts, and music and sound.

Degrees may be based in music colleges or music or engineering departments at universities, depending on the content. Some are technical and concentrate on the practical skills of sound engineering, whereas others are a mixture of music and music technology; many require some competence in performing music at certain levels. They may be entitled BMus, BSc, BEng or BA degrees depending on the content. As you might imagine, the BEng courses are for those wishing to become audio engineers and designers of electronic instruments, studio equipment and music systems. There are related, specialised courses in live sound engineering, sound and music for games, contemporary music production and sound engineering and production.

There is a list of courses accredited by the Association of Professional Recording Services (APRS) available on their education website, JAMES (Joint Audio Media Education Services); see Sources of information. The courses are accredited if they meet industry needs, so could help you get employment after you graduate.

Degree subject combinations

Music technology combines well with music, performing arts and media courses. There are specialist combinations available with electronic engineering, music performance, pop music performance, radio broadcasting and video production. You could consider combinations with management or computer science and you will also find music technology combined with science subjects.

Other higher education qualifications

Foundation degrees are available in music technology, creative audio technology, creative sound technology, creative music production, music technology and production, DJ and electronic production, media production, music production and creative recording, music performance technology and sound and music technology.

There are HNDs and HNCs in music technology, live sounds and events, music production, music performance and technology, and urban and electronic music.

Relevance to other subjects?

Depending on your interests you could consider popular, commercial music or media studies. There are also sound engineering and electronics courses. If you are interested in the music business, there are courses in music industry management and music journalism.

Important advice

Music technology degrees vary in their content and specialism, so you must research the different courses to find out which is the best for you. Course requirements also vary, as well as the standard of musical performance required, so be sure to contact universities and colleges directly to find out what would be suitable for you. It is also important to ask them what sorts of jobs their graduates go into.

Future careers

After A levels

You might start as a junior in a recording studio, or as a runner or messenger in the music or TV industries. You might find work in a radio station, the film industry, assisting with live sound at concerts and the theatre, or possibly administration work with music and other media publications. There would also be opportunities in music, computer or electronics shops. (See also the information under this heading in the music entry.) Sound and music technology apprenticeships are available and cover all areas of the music industry including the business side (See Sources of information). There are also Higher Apprenticeships in broadcast production and broadcast technology.

After a degree

Working in music technology

Depending on the content of your degree, here are some of the careers you could consider:

- audio production
- audio sales
- audio systems maintenance
- broadcast (radio, television, internet)
- equipment design
- events management
- independent musical composition and performance
- live sound production/engineering (gigs, theatre, events)
- media production
- multimedia authoring
- music education: teaching, lecturing, research, technical support
- music for digital media (interactive games, the web)
- music for time-based media (film, video)
- music production
- music technology journalism
- recording artist
- research and development
- software design
- sound capture (sound engineering)
- sound design
- sound design and post-production for film, television and radio
- studio engineering/ studio management
- television and radio engineering and production.

Some of these areas cross over into the more creative aspects of music. Some of these jobs are freelance and/or on short-term contracts, so you may end up self-employed.

Working outside music technology

You would have knowledge of IT and engineering so you could consider working in the IT or engineering industries, which might require further training. If you have a strong interest in the music industry, there could be opportunities in music management and administration, arts administration, journalism and marketing.

Sources of information

Association of Professional Recording Services (APRS)
www2.aprs.co.uk

BPI
www.bpi.co.uk

www.ccskills.org.uk/careers

www.jamesonline.org.uk   (for list of accredited higher and further education courses)

www.musictechstudent.co.uk

www.soundonsound.com (online magazine)

www.ukmusic.org/skills-academy/apprenticeships

www.bigcreative.education/bcap-vacancies

> 'A level music technology has enabled me to learn how to record my band in a professional way and given me the skills to mix music properly.'
> James, studying music technology, business and computer science A levels

PHILOSOPHY

If you have ever seen The Matrix film trilogy and wondered about some of the issues raised by the films, you will already have had an introduction to some of the key questions studied in philosophy. Why are we here? What is the truth? Do we just fit in with the way things are or question them? If you have watched the Walking Dead or The Returned series this may well have thrown up similar questions.

The word 'philosophy' comes from the ancient Greek word meaning 'love of wisdom'. The Greeks founded philosophy and the issues they considered are still studied by philosophers today. As an A level philosophy student you will be introduced to philosophical ways of thinking. You will ask philosophical questions, explore and critically engage with ideas, while making and sharpening distinctions and criticising and reinterpreting the arguments of philosophers. The skills that you will develop through your study of philosophy, such as arguing logically and lateral thinking, are extremely relevant to our information-based economy and are transferable to many other academic subjects.

What do you study?

You gain a thorough grounding in the key concepts and methods of philosophy You will strengthen your capacity for analysis, reasoning and judgement; spot flaws in logic; learn how to argue logically and confidently; understand views different from your own; and be able to oppose others' arguments.

The new specification includes female philosophers' theories and texts as well as the opportunity to engage with some of the major questions of philosophy from a secular (non-religious) viewpoint.

➢ **Epistemology** – this is the study of the nature of knowledge, the rationality of belief, and justification. Do we know anything for certain? Is there any difference between knowledge and belief? You will look at theories of different types of knowledge. You look at 'perception' as a source of knowledge, 'reason' and the limits of knowledge.

➢ **Moral philosophy** – are there moral truths and if so what is their nature?

➢ **Normative ethical theories** – the meaning of good, bad, right and wrong within each of the three approaches: utilitarianism, Kantian deontological ethics and Aristotelian virtue ethics. You will be asked to do some applied ethics and apply the normative ethical theories you have learned to issues such as stealing, simulated killing (within computer games, plays, films etc), eating animals and telling lies. You will also study meta-ethics, the branch of ethics that seeks to understand the nature of ethical properties, statements, attitudes, and judgements.

> **Metaphysics** – the branch of philosophy responsible for the study of existence, dealing with the first principles of things, including abstract concepts such as being, knowing, identity, time and space.

- **The metaphysics of God** – what is the nature of God? Is God, all-powerful and all-knowing. Does God have unlimited goodness? Different theories and arguments for the existence of God from classical times up to the present day. The problem of evil.
- **The metaphysics of mind** – what is the mind? What is its place in nature? What is the relationship between the mental and physical? How are mental states identified, experienced and known?

> **Philosophical texts** – you will study set philosophy texts as they apply to the area of philosophy outlined above. You will need to be familiar with the texts and will be required to develop and explore the problem areas identified within them. You will be expected to use this knowledge as a springboard for wider discussion and engagement of issues, and apply your acquired knowledge to philosophical problems raised in the text.

The texts are taken from a wide range of works by, for example, Aquinas, Aristotle, Bentham, Block, Chalmers, Descartes, Hare, Hume, Kant, Locke, Mill, Plato, Smart and Russell. Female philosophers including Linda Zagzebski, Julia Annas, Cora Diamond and Philippa Foot.

There is no GCSE in philosophy, however, for the study of this subject at A level you will need an enquiring and open mind, as well as the ability to write in good, clear English.

Class discussion based on your reading is an important aspect of studying philosophy, as it has been for hundreds of years. Be prepared for the reading to be difficult at first, until you get used to the way that philosophical arguments are presented. There may also be the preparation and delivery of student presentations and group topics. As you might expect, your written work will be in the form of essays and you will be expected to undertake a lot of independent study. You must be able to work hard to grasp some difficult concepts and then be able to cope with class discussions that will test your understanding and your viewpoint.

There is no coursework for philosophy A level.

Subject combinations

You are unlikely to be asked for particular A level subjects if you apply for a university course in philosophy, although mathematics may be a preference for courses involving formal logic. Otherwise, your ability to form logical arguments would be helped, and in turn reinforced, by studying subjects such as English, history, politics, psychology and religious studies.

Higher education options

It is not necessary to have an A level in philosophy in order to study it at a higher level.

Degree-level study

Philosophy degree courses vary a great deal in content. Some place a great deal of emphasis on the traditional study of the great philosophers of the past, such as Aristotle, Plato and Descartes. Others focus on modern issues relating to politics, psychology, education and religion. All of them encourage you to form and defend your own ideas. Most courses begin with a year spent introducing you to the main strands in philosophical argument and other courses are even broader to begin with, starting with a general foundation course covering other humanities subjects as well as philosophy.

As you progress through the course you will find yourself with an increasing number of options, with some third years having no compulsory topics.

Options could include history and the philosophy of science, feminist philosophy (theories about the position of women in society), aesthetics (how we judge beauty and art), the philosophy of time, the philosophy of time travel, the philosophy of maths or the works of particular philosophers such as Kant Hegel, Nietzsche or Wittgenstein. Some degrees specialise in computing philosophy, European philosophy, natural philosophy, mental philosophy or world philosophies. Some courses offer a work or study placement.

Degree subject combinations

On many courses you have the option of continuing to study philosophy alongside another subject, and there is a wide range of subjects in the arts, humanities and sciences. There are also several degrees combining three subjects: philosophy, politics, economics (PPE). These degree programmes are designed so that the subjects throw light on each other. Other popular combinations are politics, economics, religious studies, history and modern languages.

Other higher education qualifications

As foundation degrees are vocational, there are none in philosophy. You might want to consider those available in law, politics or community studies.

There are no HNDs or HNCs in philosophy although an HND in legal studies or business law is one possibility, as it gives you plenty of opportunity to use your experience of logical argument and can provide the foundation for a career in law.

Relevance to other subjects?

Philosophy helps you to think about and understand important and complex ideas and issues, and encourages you to look at them critically and sensibly. You will be able to use ideas from present-day thought as well as evidence taken from the works of thinkers throughout history. This experience would provide a good basis for many subjects, including politics, law, theology/religious studies, economics, history, sociology, linguistics, drama and classics. Also look at subjects like human rights or international relations.

Important advice

You cannot be a lazy thinker in philosophy and your commitment to the subject will be clear from the amount of reading that you do. Interviews for higher level philosophy courses often involve discussion of what you have read, not just the books on the set texts for your A level subject. The more you read in philosophy, the better you will become at forming intelligent arguments of your own.

Future careers

After A levels

Philosophy is not a vocational subject so won't lead straight into a particular career. It does help you to become a clear and critical thinker who can put together a reasoned, intelligent argument. These skills are valuable to employers in many areas, including administration or any job requiring organisational skills. You would be an effective member of any team where the powers of persuasive argument are important such as in marketing or sales.

After a degree

Working in philosophy

Careers linked directly to philosophy are limited as there are very few full-time philosophers. The nearest you might get to working as a philosopher is by teaching or lecturing in schools, colleges or universities.

If you want to teach in a state school you will need to offer an additional National Curriculum subject such as history, or politics, as well as undertaking further training to gain QTS (Qualified Teacher Status).

Only if you become a philosophy lecturer or writer will you get the chance actually to 'do some philosophy' of your own. This could involve further study at postgraduate level.

Working outside philosophy

Most philosophy graduates go on to work in areas that enable them to use their ability to ask intelligent questions, analyse a problem and come up with a reasoned decision. Many philosophy graduates find employment in management or administration, where the ability to make informed decisions (often on other people's behalf) is extremely important. Others use their powers of argument in sales, advertising and marketing, targeting potential buyers for a product and finding the most effective way of selling it. Financial jobs are also a possibility as are jobs in law or politics. Some graduates go on to work in journalism, the media, publishing or social work.

Sources of information

Royal Institute of Philosophy
www.royalinstitutephilosophy.org

British Philosophical Association
www.bpa.ac.uk

www.alevelphilosophy.co.uk

www.philosophynow.org

www.philosophyofreligion.info

'I like recruiting philosophy graduates as their philosophy degree has trained their brain and given them the ability to provide the skills we require and clients demand. These skills include the ability to be analytical, provide clear and innovative thinking, and question assumptions.'
Russell, director of a management consultancy

PHYSICAL EDUCATION

Studying physical education gives you the opportunity to develop a theoretical understanding of the physiological, psychological and sociological factors that underpin sporting performance as well as gaining practical experience and evaluating your own performance. Sport and exercise is a huge, and rapidly-expanding, global industry, while levels of public health, fitness and participation in physical activity are issues on the political agenda. The specifications focus on participation and performance in physical activity as part of a balanced, active and healthy lifestyle. The new specs have an increased focus on quantitative skills, data analysis and the use of new technology in sport. They also have an increased range of sports available including para-sports.

What do you study?

The topics listed give an idea of what could be covered. The exact content of specifications differs according to exam boards. You will need to check with your school or college about the exact options available to you.

➤ **Applied anatomy and physiology** – the cardiovascular system, respiratory system, neuromuscular system, musculoskeletal system and the body's energy systems.

➤ **Factors affecting performance in physical activity and sport** – exercise physiology, diet and nutrition, preparation and training methods, injury prevention and the rehabilitation of injury. Understanding of the changes within the body systems prior to exercise, during exercise of differing intensities and during recovery.

➤ **Biomechanical movement** – understanding the action of external and internal forces on the living body, especially on the skeletal system, and their relevance to performance in physical activity and sport.

➤ **Sports psychology** – understanding the psychological factors that can affect performance in physical activity and sport; the individual differences affecting people in physical activity and sport; group and team dynamics in sport; the importance of goal setting in sports performance; the role of attribution in motivating performers; confidence and self-efficacy in sport; leadership in sport and stress management in physical activities and sports to optimise performance.

➤ **Sport and society** – the history of sport and how it has evolved, how social and cultural factors shaped the development of, and participation, in sport. The nature of global sporting events such as the modern Olympic Games and how they reflect and are impacted upon by social issues. Routes to sporting excellence in the UK. How talent can be spotted and developed. The role of UK Sport and other organisations in increasing participation in sport. The factors that shape contemporary sport.

➢ **Contemporary issues** – such as doping, gambling in sport, commercialisation e.g. sponsorship, the media. How modern technology has impacted on sport, monitoring safety and health, fairer judging (such as goal-line technology), replays.

Practical

30% of the A level is practical assessment of either playing or coaching a sport. The designated sports are: amateur boxing, association football, athletics, badminton, basketball, camogie, canoeing, cricket, cycling, dance, diving, Gaelic football, golf, gymnastics, handball, hockey, equestrian, hurling, kayaking, lacrosse, netball, rock climbing, rowing, rugby league, rugby union, sculling, skiing, snowboarding, squash, swimming, table tennis, tennis, trampolining, volleyball and specialist sports: blind cricket, boccia, goal ball, powerchair football, polybat, table cricket, wheelchair basketball, wheelchair rugby.

Quantitative, research and data analysis skills

The new specifications require that students develop these skills to be able to further their knowledge and understanding of physical education. You will learn to interpret data to look at, for example, changes within musculoskeletal, cardiorespiratory and neuromuscular systems during different types of physical activity and sport. You will need a good grasp of quantitative methods for planning, monitoring and evaluating physical training and performance. You will also need to use equations, formulae and units of measurement to plot, label and interpret graphs and diagrams. The assessment of these skills represents a minimum of 5% of the overall A level and AS level marks.

It is not necessary to have taken GCSE physical education in order to study this A level. However, if you have taken this GCSE course and/or biology, you may find it useful in the transition to A level work.

Subject combinations

If you are considering a degree in physical education, sports science or sports and exercise science, then either biology, chemistry, physics or psychology would be useful to support your application and a science is required for some courses. Physical education A level also goes well with subjects such as history and sociology. If you are considering sports or leisure management, business or maths A levels would be good choices.

Higher education options

Degree-level study

There are three main areas involved in studying physical education/sports science at degree level:

- sports psychology
- exercise physiology – nutrition, diet etc.
- sport biomechanics – the analysis of physiology during sporting activities.

Within these you will find a variety of modules, examples are: anatomy, professional and academic skills for sport, data analysis in sport and exercise, applied exercise physiology, exercise prescription and instruction, cognition and emotion in sport and exercise psychology, research in sport and exercise, performance analysis, applied strength and conditioning, working with a client, professional issues in sport and exercise psychology, applied performance analysis, teaching and coaching, sport management, professional development and employability.

Some courses will include a work placement and some offer the chance to gain National Governing Body qualifications in a variety of sports. Some also offer a placement year in the UK or overseas which might be with a sports team, sporting organisation, sports company or a university.

There are specialised degrees available, such as sports and exercise science, physical education and coaching, sports coaching, sport rehabilitation, nutrition (exercise and health), sport therapy, sports conditioning, rehabilitation and massage, marine sports science, and sport development. There are business-focused courses in sport management and sport business management. Some of degrees specialise in a particular sport. There are also physical education degrees incorporating teacher training. If you are considering sports psychology, you must choose a degree that is approved by the BPS (British Psychological Society). An interesting new degree is extreme sports engineering.

Degree subject combinations

You can combine sports science or sports studies with related subjects, like human biology, or with management courses, such as tourism, leisure or outdoor studies. You could also consider combinations with business, ICT or languages.

Other higher education qualifications

Foundation degrees include outdoor adventure leadership and management, marine sport science, coaching, outdoor fitness, community sport coaching, personal training, sports therapy and injury rehabilitation,

Specialist foundation degrees are available in cricket coaching, football coaching, football business management and coaching, rugby coaching and development, equine sports coaching, golf management, and golf coaching and performance. You could consider related degrees in sport and leisure management, sports journalism, sport management, sports surface management or surf science and technology.

HND courses available include sports studies, sports coaching, sport and exercise science, sports therapy, sports development and coaching, and sports and leisure management.

Relevance to other subjects?

Look at courses in leisure and recreation management and in hotel and hospitality management. You could also consider courses in psychology or sociology, youth work or teaching.

Important advice

In order to keep up with the practical component of the course you should follow a training regime (or continue with any existing programme that you may have).This should include general cardiovascular work together with some resistance training. A general pattern of healthy living, such as a healthy diet excluding cigarettes and alcohol, is regarded as essential. If you have done any related work experience (such as helping in a secondary school PE department) or have any coaching experience or qualifications, make sure you mention this on your UCAS personal statement.

Future careers

After A levels

A knowledge of physical education could help you work within the sports and leisure industry in roles such as a leisure centre assistant. You might also consider sports coaching, lifeguard or personal fitness instruction work (depending on any extra qualifications you may have gained). Your knowledge of anatomy and physiology would be useful in healthcare jobs. Working in retail sports shops or jobs in IT and administration connected to the sports industry could also be options. The National School Apprenticeship scheme offers apprenticeships in schools, some specialising in sport. There are Advanced Level Apprenticeships in sports coaching, personal training and leisure and recreation management which could help you break into the industry.

After a degree

Working in physical education

About one in five sports science graduates go into professional jobs in sports straight after graduating.

➢ **Health and fitness industry** – this is a major career option for sports studies graduates so you might consider a career in the management of fitness, leisure centres, health clubs or spas. You might start as a personal trainer, which can offer a good route into the industry. You may also find jobs in local or national government such as an active lifestyles officer or health adviser promoting healthy living and lifestyles in the community.

➢ **Coaching** – this ranges from coaching elite sportspeople for high-level activities (such as the Olympics) to providing for the needs of young people in the community. It also connects with the popular world of personal development training, especially in large corporate companies. Local councils are increasingly recognising the need for young people to be able to access sporting facilities, and the need for professional coaching in this area is now widely acknowledged.

➢ **Exercise physiologist** – providing scientific support at various levels to athletes and teams within a single sport or several sports. They are employed by sports organisations and in research centres, academic institutions, hospitals and medical centres. They may work in a sports setting or within the NHS as a clinical exercise physiologist.

➢ **Sports development officer** – promoting sports locally within the community, often targeted at a particular group, for example young people. You would work for local or national government or possibly a charity.

➢ **Teaching** – you would need to undertake further training to gain QTS (Qualified Teacher Status) unless you choose a course which includes education and qualified teacher status.

➢ **Outdoor activities manager or leader** – managing an outdoor activities centre, offering instruction to a wide range of people, or becoming a leader where you offer people instruction and encouragement.

➢ **Sports marketing and media** – this ranges from being an events manager and being involved with the general business of putting on events, to gaining sponsorship or becoming an agent for sportspeople. This often involves establishing links with the corporate and business world and is a developing area.

➢ **Sport psychologist** – studying the mental and emotional effects of taking part in sport and exercise. There are sports psychology first degrees but it is also possible to qualify with a sports science degree or equivalent by taking a postgraduate course. You must make sure that the course is accredited by the BPS.

➢ **Physiotherapy** - sports science graduates or equivalent need to take a pre-registration postgraduate course to qualify as a physiotherapist.

➢ **Postgraduate study** – just under 14% of sports science graduates go on to further study, in areas such as in sports studies, health and exercise nutrition, sports biomechanics, sports performance, physiotherapy, psychology and human resources.

Working outside physical education

Your degree could equip you a wide range of careers such as management, finance, social services, the police, the fire service and the Armed Forces.

Sources of information

British Association of Sport and Exercise Sciences
www.bases.org.uk

British Sports
www.britishsports.com

Sport England
www.sportengland.org

Sportscotland
www.sportscotland.org.uk

Sport Wales
www.sportwales.org.uk

UK Sport
www.uksport.gov.uk

Careers in sport
www.careers-in-sport.co.uk

National School Apprenticeship Programme
www.schoolapprenticeships.co.uk

www.healthcareers.nhs.uk for physiotherapy and exercise physiologist
information

SkillsActive
www.skillsactive.com

> *'It's such a satisfying job. I organised some 'Walking for health walks' locally. It got people out of their cars and provided a chance to experience the health benefits of a short stroll.'*
> Doug, active lifestyles officer, with a degree in sport studies

PHYSICS

Physics is unique. No other subject allows you to gain such a deep understanding of the way the world works. It can stretch to study of space and universe but is also down to earth and includes items that we take for granted in the modern world like mobile phones, the internet, PCs and the power that runs them. It is an exciting and creative science, which is constantly evolving as new discoveries are made.

Studying physics is all about observing natural phenomena, trying to understand them and predicting what might happen in new and unknown situations. You learn about a wide range of theories explaining and predicting the way in which the physical world behaves. Physics is continually developing with new theories and practical techniques, so offers a unique base from which to meet the demands of new technologies in our ever-changing world. This also means that the range of careers and opportunities is ever-growing.

The new specifications have an emphasis on the maths skills required for the study of physics and some new topics such as space and particle physics.

What do you study?

The topics listed give an idea of what could be covered. The exact content of specifications differs according to exam boards. You will need to check with your school or college about the exact options available to you.

➢ **the properties of matter** – solids, liquids and gases; mechanical, thermal and electrical properties explained in molecular terms

➢ **the properties of materials** – including density and Young's modulus

➢ **mechanics** – including motion along a straight line, projectile motion, Newton's laws of motion, energy and power

➢ **oscillations and waves** – mechanical and electromagnetic waves, sound and optics

➢ **quantum physics** – photo electricity, energy levels and photon emission, wave-particle duality

➢ **nuclear and particle physics**

➢ **fields** – force fields, gravitational fields, electric fields, capacitors, magnetic fields, electromagnetic induction, particle accelerators, fundamental particles

➢ **electricity** – electrical quantities, resistance and resistivity, circuits and components, alternating current, direct current circuits

> **further mechanics** – including momentum, circular motion and simple harmonic motion

> **development of practical skills** – skills of planning, implementing, analysis and evaluation

> **other topics** – you may also study a range of other topics, including space, nuclear radiation, gravitational fields, engineering physics, the development of physics, electronics, medical physics, thermal physics, astrophysics and applied physics. This will depend on the specification.

There are also physics A level specifications driven by real-life applications, focusing on the practical activities and applications of physics. An example is advancing physics.

You learn through a combination of theory and practical work. Theory is taught through lectures explaining conceptual physical models. You develop your understanding of much of the theory by applying it to increasingly complex problems, and you will be expected to read textbooks and scientific journals to increase your understanding. Practical work is used to learn experimental techniques, to place the theory in context and to help develop a deeper understanding of physical phenomena. You will learn the selection and use of different types of equipment, processing of data, making observations and measurements, and the analysis and evaluation of results.

A good grade (C or above or grade 4 or better with new GCSEs) in physics or science and additional science at GCSE is usually required to study A level physics. You will also need to be able to use mathematical formulae confidently.

Maths
40% of the A level marks in the written exams will assess the use of maths skills as they relate to physics. The standard is Level 2 or above so equivalent to the standard of the higher tier GCSE maths.

Practical assessment
For A level, students need to demonstrate confidence in practical techniques. For AS level, this will be assessed by written exam. For A level, the practical assessments are divided into those that can be assessed in written exams and those that can only be directly assessed by carrying out experiments. A level grades are based only on marks from written exams. A separate endorsement of practical skills is taken with the A level. This is assessed by teachers and will be based on direct observation of students' competency in a range of skills that are not assessable in written exams. A minimum of 12 practical activities are

assessed (not under exam conditions). There is a single pass grade which will be on the A level certificate.

Subject combinations

Physics combines well with other science subjects, but maths will be particularly helpful and relevant as there is so much maths involved in physics. You should take A level mathematics if you are thinking of a degree in a physics subject or engineering. Further maths is useful for some engineering courses, such as aeronautical engineering. Physics A level combines well with chemistry, leading to medical courses and many technology and science-based courses including medical engineering, materials engineering and textile science and technology.

Physics could also be combined with A level design and technology for engineering design or product design courses. If you are considering chemical engineering, you must take chemistry A level.

If you did not take the right subjects for entry to an undergraduate physics degree, there are foundation years available for some courses, which are designed to fill gaps in maths and physics and prepare you for entry onto the first year of a degree.

Higher education options

Degree-level study

Traditional physics courses give you a solid grounding for the first two years in modern and classical physics along with the associated mathematics and experimental techniques. Important areas covered include dynamics, mechanics, relativity, quantum physics, electromagnetism, waves and optics, atomic and nuclear physics, particle physics, oscillations, thermodynamics, lasers and solid-state physics. In the third year there is the opportunity to specialise from a wide range of options including: atomic and molecular structure, solid state electronic devices, electro-magnetic radiation, lasers, stars and cosmology, particle and nuclear physics and the more advanced aspects of theoretical physics.

Maths features in all physics courses, both as a language through which physics is expressed and as a method for the development of the subject and for problem solving. If the maths side of physics particularly appeals to you then you could consider a degree in theoretical physics.

Four-year courses lead to the qualification of MPhys or MSci and aim for the greater subject depth you need if you want to practise as a physicist in research or in industry.

Some physics degrees are sandwich courses, which involve placements in industry or study abroad. Placements could be with a wide variety of employers or research establishments, for example BAE, the National Physical Laboratory or National Oceanography Centre. Or your placement could be abroad, for example at the high-energy research centre (CERN) in Geneva, the WSL– the Swiss Federal Institute for Forest, Snow and Landscape Research in Davos, or the Max Planck Institutes in Germany.

Degree subject combinations

You can combine physics with virtually any subject, although some subjects are closely related, like electronics, astronomy or mathematics. If you think you might not want a purely technical career, combining physics with management, business studies, ICT or a modern language would be a good preparation for careers in management, business or industry.

Other higher education qualifications

There are foundation degrees available in physics and also specialist degrees in shortage areas such as nuclear engineering (decommissioning), nuclear engineering (power generation) and clinical technology. These could lead into linked degree courses or employment. There are no HNDs or HNCs in pure physics but in related areas: biological and chemical sciences and engineering.

Relevance to other subjects?

Physics A level is useful for many related degrees, such as engineering, materials science, nuclear engineering or geophysics. There are also courses in engineering physics, which are designed to combine education and training in the branches of physics that have been identified as important for the development of a professional engineer. It is also useful for entry to medicine, dentistry and veterinary science. The mathematical basis of physics makes it a good preparation for many other subjects. For example, there is increasing emphasis upon scientific research methods and statistical analysis in courses such as psychology, sociology, economics and business studies, so there are many options.

Important advice

Have a look at the content of courses to see which ones inspire you. There could be sponsorship or bursaries for physics or engineering degrees. This is competitive, and sometimes the closing dates are before the UCAS closing dates.

Future careers

After A levels

There are many Higher and Degree Apprenticeships available enabling you to obtain higher level qualifications while working.

Examples are advanced manufacturing engineering in areas such as aerospace, the nuclear industry, mechanical and electrical engineering, wind generation, research and development, marine, space and rail engineering. Also engineering environmental technologies with specialisms in construction and the built environment and building services engineer. You could look at life sciences and chemical sciences apprenticeships which include training routes for chemical science and for work as a technologist, life sciences technologist and healthcare science technologist. There are also apprenticeships in manufacturing such as in process development, packaging technology and food science. Laboratory science apprenticeships are another possibility.

Having studied physics, you will have good problem-solving, research and report-writing skills, so you could consider Higher and Degree Apprenticeships in many other career areas including business and finance.

After a degree

Working in physics

Physics graduates can use their particular skills and knowledge in working for a wide range of employers including:

➤ **engineering and electronic companies** – researching and developing new products

➤ **utilities providers** – particularly telecommunications, power and transport

➤ **energy** – this could be in traditional fields, such as gas, oil and electricity, improving fuel efficiency and output, or research into new or renewable sources like wind and wave power

➤ **medical physics** – magnetic resonance imaging (MRI) scanners, lasers used in surgery, ultrasound, therapeutic radiography for treating cancer

➤ **materials industries** – including steel, plastics and ceramics producers and companies using these materials

➤ **radiation protection** – monitoring emissions and ensuring the safe disposal of radioactive waste. This could be within Public Health England

➤ **defence** – employed by agencies and contractors of the Ministry of Defence, you might design and implement new weapons systems and technology, and intelligence systems (e.g. through communication satellites)

➤ **space science** – researching other planets, building satellites and space probes, collecting information about the universe and its origins

➤ **schools and colleges** – physics teachers are in demand, and there is extra financial help available for teacher training in science subjects

➤ **research** – in research scientist jobs for government departments and commercial companies.

Many physics graduates move on to further study after their first degree (just over a third), taking courses such as PhDs and MScs in subjects such as accelerator physics, applied mathematics, astrophysics, nanotechnology, nuclear engineering, audio acoustics, radio imaging, computer software technology with network management, information technology, plasma physics and radiation detection. It is possibly for physics graduates to take a four-year graduate course to qualify in medicine.

Working outside physics

Physics is a subject providing strong academic and technical training. The IT industry employs many physics graduates as software engineers, programmers, systems analysts and IT consultants. As a physics graduate you could enter a wide variety of careers including accountancy, technical sales and marketing, banking, finance, or local and national government.

Sources of information

Institute of Physics
www.iop.org

Careers in physics
www.physics.org/careers

Science Museum
www.sciencemuseum.org.uk

Search for physics courses
www.myphysicscourse.org

www.physlink.com

'A physics degree teaches you how to think. I enjoy the problem-solving and how maths becomes so relevant and important in this subject.'
Brigid, BSc physics

POLITICS

Politics affects our everyday lives. The results of national and local elections have far-reaching consequences in our lives as they influence education, health, defence and, on a local level, even how frequently our dustbins are emptied. We need to understand how politics works if we are to play a full role as a citizen in our democracy.

Politics is about much more than who is going to win the next general election. As a student of A level politics you will explore how political power is gained and used, and learn about how governments and other political institutions and systems work both in the UK, USA and globally. You look at political structures, such as the voting system and Parliament, and the case for and against changing those structures; the definitions and the functions of concepts such as democracy, justice and rights; and recent developments in the world of politics. The specifications require you to critically analyse and evaluate the areas of politics you study in order to construct arguments and explanations leading to reasoned conclusions. They also encourage you to identify parallels, connections, similarities and differences between aspects of the areas of politics studied. The new specifications include global politics as a new option.

What do you study?

The topics listed give an idea of what could be covered. The exact content of specifications differs according to exam boards. You will need to check with your school or college about the exact options available to you.

For the A level, you will study government in the UK and then one of either comparative politics: government and politics of the USA, or global politics.

GOVERNMENT IN THE UK

You gain a broad understanding of the UK political system, including the role of elections, political parties and pressure groups, voter behaviour, the role of the media and how policy is made. This includes the British constitution, the structure, role and powers of Parliament and how it works and is accountable. You will also look at the impact of devolution on the UK, including the different roles and powers of the Scottish Parliament and Government, the Welsh Assembly and Government, and the Northern Ireland Assembly and Executive, as well as devolution in England.

➤ **Political participation in the UK** – democracy and participation – how democracy has evolved. Elections and voting – examining different general elections, how they operate, voting patterns, the impact of referendums.

➤ **Political parties** – the origin of different political parties, how they operate and influence policy.

> **The European Union** – its role and relationship with the UK.

> **Political ideas** – liberalism, conservatism, socialism, nationalism, feminism, multiculturalism, anarchism, ecologism.

COMPARATIVE POLITICS: GOVERNMENT AND POLITICS OF THE USA

You will look at different approaches to the study of comparative politics: structural, rational and cultural, including the different ways they explain similarities and differences between the government and politics of different countries, and the extent to which they explain these similarities and differences in the UK and USA. You will cover the constitution of the USA, Congress, the President, the Supreme Court, democracy and participation and civil rights.

GLOBAL POLITICS

This option gives you knowledge and understanding of the key concepts, structures of and influences on global politics as well as current global issues, such as conflict, poverty, human rights and the environment.

> **Global government** – the origins and development of international law in creating the concept of global politics, the origins, development and role of major global institutions, including the United Nations.

You will examine institutions of global political governance: the UN and other key bodies; the North Atlantic Treaty Organisation (NATO); institutions of global economic governance: the International Monetary Fund (IMF), World Bank, World Trade Organization (WTO) and the Group of Eight; institutions of global environmental governance including the UN Framework Convention on Climate Change (UNFCCC).

> **Developments in global politics** – different systems of government including democratic, semi-democratic, nondemocratic and autocratic states.

The changing nature of world order since 2000 and the implications of conditions including bipolarity, unipolarity and multipolarity.

The differing significance of states in global affairs, and why some states are classified as great powers or superpowers (USA) and emerging powers, including BRICS (Brazil, Russia, India, China and South Africa).The use and effectiveness of different types of power including military action, diplomacy and cultural activity. The development and spread of liberal economies, the rule of law, and democracy (for example South Korea, Taiwan, Singapore).

> **Globalisation** – the processes of globalisation and its impact on the states system, the factors driving globalisation (economic, cultural, political, social and technological), the impact of globalisation, its advantages and disadvantages, and particularly its implications for the nation state and national sovereignty, the ways and extent to which globalisation addresses and resolves contemporary global issues, such as those involving conflict, poverty, human rights and the environment.

> **Regionalism** – debates about the reasons for, and significance of, region-alisation, the factors that have fostered European integration, and the major developments through which this has occurred (economic and monetary union), the process of enlargement, and the significance of the EU as an international body; the development of other regional organisations including the North American Free Trade Association (NAFTA), the African Union (AU), the Arab League and the Association of Southeast Asian Nations (ASEAN).

All these are studied in the context of current and recent issues, arguments and events. A GCSE in the subject is not required for study at A level but you must be enthusiastic about politics and have a good grasp of English.

You study through lessons, discussions and research tasks and may take part in mock elections or 'Question Time' sessions. You may listen to invited speakers, visit political organisations, the House of Commons or even Washington DC. You will be expected to keep up-to-date with current events.

Subject combinations

Universities generally do not ask for any specific A levels for entry to degrees in government, politics or related subjects but some do have 'preferred' subjects. Useful A levels include history, philosophy, geography, English, economics, law and sociology.

Higher education options

Degree-level study

There is a wide range of politics degrees and many have their own particular focus. You will also find there are specialist degrees in international politics, political economy, international relations and a degree entitled elections, public opinions and parties at the University of Essex. Many degrees offer a work placement.

The main areas of study are:

> **British politics** – constitutional reforms and the devolution/independence of Scotland, Wales and Northern Ireland. Britain and the EU, the euro and the sovereignty debate.

> **global politics** – comparing European and British systems and other political systems. Many universities offer courses focusing on the politics of other countries or regions such as the USA, the Middle East, Latin America, Asia, Africa or Australasia.

> **political theory** – where you consider key questions about the nature of freedom and the strengths and limitations of democracy. The relationship between government and society, the right of dissent and the limits of toleration, and questions of social justice and equality.

> **elections** – and how they can change the course of a country. Studying elections can be about predicting results, trying to work out why people vote as they do, or even why they don't vote at all. Party campaigns, what policies are put forward and how parties select candidates. The effect of social media on political campaigns and public participation and opinion.

> **international relations** – covers topics such as the role of international organisations (such as the United Nations), the strategies of various politicians on the international political stage, the role of international non-governmental organisations (for example large corporations) and vital international policy areas like the environment. It addresses questions such as why wars occur, how peace is negotiated and maintained, and international justice.

There are many other options such as researching politics, the history of political thought, media, journalism and society, identity politics, political consumerism, social media, online political participation and the role of the media in shaping our political perspectives and experiences, digital politics: the impact of emerging digital technologies in communications strategies and campaigns, political psychology, political marketing and campaigning, youth culture and politics, the Cold War, women and equal rights, security studies and human rights.

On many courses you can spend some time on fieldwork and this might involve working with a political party or pressure group, or you may even go abroad, observing the work of the European Parliament, European Commission or NATO.

Degree subject combinations

Politics is available in combination with business, economics, history, philosophy, sociology, law and languages. There are also combinations with subjects like globalisation, human rights, international relations, conflict studies or social policy.

Other higher education qualifications

There are no foundation degrees available in politics but there are some in related topics, such as community leadership and public services. You might want to look at related courses in public services and legal studies. These are more vocational than degree courses and aim to prepare you for careers in public services or as a paralegal. (For more information on paralegals, see the entry for law.)

There are no HNDs or HNCs available in politics but there are related courses in legal studies, business law, public services and public and emergency services.

Relevance to other subjects?

Politics A level gives you skills in how to develop ideas and arguments backed up with reliable evidence. This will be useful in many other subjects, especially economics, philosophy, law and history.

Important advice

You must get into the habit of reading a quality newspaper regularly and keeping in touch with current events and issues. Applying what you learn to real-world events will make your studies far more interesting and give you a head start over other students, especially if you decide to apply for politics courses at degree level.

Future careers

After A levels

It may be possible to get into jobs in national or local government. The study of politics increases your awareness of what is going on in the world and develops your skills of argument and discussion (both written and spoken), which can be used in many areas. Politics affects the work of the police and customs services, so an appreciation of issues such as immigration, civil liberties, and protest and pressure groups would be helpful in these careers. There are Higher Apprenticeships in business and professional administration which will help you enter these areas of work and the Civil Service has a Fast Track Apprenticeship scheme.

After a degree

Working in politics

➢ **Elected politicians** – you usually start off by working unpaid for a political party, whether at a local or national level, and are then selected by the party to stand at an election for a council seat or parliamentary constituency.

➢ **Agents and researchers** – some people enter politics by becoming an agent for an MP (they are usually in the political party first) and there are opportunities to become researchers or assistants to MPs (or their equivalents in the devolved UK parliaments).

➢ **Political consultants and lobbyists** – employed by companies or other groups that want to see a particular issue raised and examined in Parliament.

➢ **Local government officers** – work at a local level in areas such as housing, highways and other public facilities.

➢ **Civil servants** – if you reach the senior grades in the Civil Service, you will be advising government ministers on how policy should be put into practice. Recruitment to the senior Civil Service is through intensive selection tests, after which you are assigned to a particular department such as health, defence or education.

➢ **Other related jobs** – trade union work, political party organiser the voluntary sector, including international organisations, academic teaching and research and political journalism.

Working outside politics

A degree in politics is accepted for a wide range of careers. As a politics graduate you will be able to express yourself clearly in speech and writing. This makes you an ideal candidate for work in business, the media, journalism, management or the law.

Sources of information

The Political Studies Association
www.psa.ac.uk

Civil Service careers
https://www.gov.uk/government/organisations/civil-service/about/recruitment
includes information about Fast Track Apprenticeship and Graduate Entry

www.parliament.uk

www.w4mp.org

www.politicsresources.net

'Through my placement year in an MP's office, I've been able to gain real insight into the workings of government departments and agencies, providing me with a practical understanding of UK politics that compliments the theoretical understanding acquired on the course modules.'
Alex, with A levels in geography, history and politics, now taking a BA in politics.

PSYCHOLOGY

Psychology is the study of human experience and behaviour. It tries to help you understand both your own and others' behaviour. Why do people do the things they do, or think the way they think? How do our brains work and what influence does our environment have on our behaviour? Studying psychology will give you an insight into the human mind. You'll conduct research, discuss and debate issues and discover the work of the great pioneers in the field.

What do you study?

The topics listed give an idea of what could be covered. The exact content of specifications differs according to exam boards. You will need to check with your school or college about the exact options available to you.

The new specifications have an increased emphasis on quantitative skills (the ability to handle data and use numerical evidence systematically), data handling and scientific research methods. Some specifications offer the chance to study new options such as child psychology, criminal psychology, sports and exercise psychology and environmental psychology. There is also an increased emphasis on how psychological theory can be applied to real-world situations.

➢ **Origins of psychology** – how psychology emerged as a science

➢ **Method** – how psychologists design and conduct research and how the data is researched and analysed

➢ **Psychological concepts and theories** – learning about understanding and analysing psychological concepts, theories, research studies, research methods and ethical issues.

➢ **Social psychology** – how the individual and social forces interact

➢ **Cognitive psychology** – how we obtain, process and remember information; language and its relation to thought, including memory and eyewitness testimony

➢ **Individual differences** – personality, intelligence, normal and abnormal behaviour, mental illness and its treatments (including anxiety disorders and autism)

➢ **Biopsychology** – how our biological and physiological make-up relate to thought and behaviour; issues include motivation, emotion, awareness, sleep and stress, factors affecting stress, coping with stress and managing stress

➢ **Developmental psychology** – how we change during the course of our lives, including social and cognitive development, language acquisition, childhood, adolescence and old age

➢ **Psychopathology** – how our physical and psychological well-being may be interrelated; addictions and eating disorders, phobias, depression and obsessive-compulsive disorder (OCD)

➢ **Educational psychology** – how we learn and how this might be influenced by how we are taught

➢ **Forensic psychology** – measuring and defining crime; offender profiling, biological explanations of offending behaviour. Psychological explanations of offending behaviour; dealing with offending behaviour; behaviour modification in custody. Anger management and restorative justice programmes.

Psychology has no coursework and is examined by written exams for both AS and A level.

A GCSE in psychology is not needed to study A level psychology but you will need GCSEs at grade C or above (or grade 4 or better with the revised GCSEs) in English, mathematics and, often, a science. Maths is especially useful, because of the statistics involved in psychology and because the A level exam will assess mathematical skills at Level 2 (GCSE) or higher.

The course involves learning to evaluate arguments, write critically and think analytically. You will become familiar with experimental and other research methods, and evaluate their application to psychological hypotheses and research questions. You also need to develop structured arguments and write extensively about issues that arise in research across psychological approaches.

Subject combinations

Most degree courses do not specify particular A levels for psychology degrees, and many specify a mixture of sciences and arts with an emphasis on science. Science subjects are usually classified as physics, chemistry, biology, psychology, geography and mathematics. However, some courses involve a lot of experimental design and analysis, and mathematics and sciences are often essential. GCSE maths and English and, sometimes, a science are often essential requirements for entry to degree-level study in psychology. The main thing is to get high grades in your A levels, as psychology is a very popular and competitive degree.

Higher education options

An A level in psychology is not essential for study of the subject at a higher level.

Degree-level study

A psychology degree can be focused towards science (when it will usually be a BSc degree) or arts (usually a BA), the main difference being the amount of emphasis on experiment and quantitative analysis. A BA course will include some quantitative work but will focus more on theories and topics within psychology that rely less on statistical data or quantitative investigation. Such topics include the ethics of psychology (the potential power that a psychologist has in terms of knowledge about people's behaviour and emotions, and how this power can be abused), or theories of how we may develop particular personalities.

Instead of a straight psychology degree, you might consider a course that is more focused, such as educational, health, forensic, criminological or sports psychology. There are some broader courses available such as behavioural sciences (usually combining psychology and sociology, sometimes with animal behaviour, biology or anthropology), cognitive science (combining psychology with computer science – especially artificial intelligence, the modelling of thought processes using computers) or neuropsychology, dealing with the physical psychology of the brain and working with people with neurodegenerative diseases, tumors, strokes or brain injuries.

If you are considering becoming a psychologist, you must make sure that your course is recognised by the British Psychological Society (BPS) (see Sources of information).

Degree subject combinations

Psychology is available in many combined degree schemes, so it can be studied in combination with practically any other subject. You could consider subjects that are connected or complementary such as sociology, criminology, anthropology, sport, childhood studies or sport and exercise science. There are also less specialised combinations available such as computing, mathematics, business studies, English, geography and management.

Other higher education qualifications

There are foundation degrees available in psychology and crime, psychology and criminal behaviour, psychology and counselling, psychology and law, and psychology and health studies. For those interested in animal psychology there is foundation degree in animal behaviour and psychology as well as canine and feline training and behaviour. There is an HND in applied psychology.

Relevance to other subjects?

You will find your A level in psychology useful in other subjects at degree level. It provides grounding in research methods, analytical skills, data handling, report writing and logical problem solving, all of which will be useful for subjects such as sociology, economics and geography. If you are interested in helping people, then counselling could be another option.

Important advice

If you are considering a career in psychology, you should check that your chosen degree programme has been validated by the BPS as giving the Graduate Basis for Chartered Membership (GBC), especially if you want to work in the National Health Service. If the course that you take doesn't provide this, you may have to sit more exams after leaving university to meet the entry requirements for professional psychology training. Be aware that psychology is a very competitive subject so you will need high A level grades for entry to degree courses.

Future careers

After A levels

If you intend to go into work straight after A levels, you are likely to find that many employers value the knowledge and skills you have gained from the psychology A level. Your communication and research skills will be valuable in business, sales and marketing, the media and the health sector.

After a degree

Working in psychology

There are many options if you want to become a professional psychologist but you will need to undertake postgraduate study for nearly all of them. You are likely to have to get some practical work experience before you start your specialist postgraduate training. About 20% of psychology graduates each year go on to qualify professionally in psychology.

➤ **Clinical psychologists** work directly with patients in a hospital or as part of a community healthcare team. They may also undertake research.

➤ **Counselling psychologists** help individuals, couples, families and groups who are having problems with normal life. They help people to understand their problems and make their own decisions. They may work in GPs' surgeries, counselling organisations, academic and business settings, or privately.

➤ **Educational psychologists** work with children and young people who may have learning difficulties or behavioural problems.

➤ **Forensic (criminological and legal) psychologists** work with other professionals in the courts and prisons. Their work ranges from assessing the mental competence of offenders to participating in the day-to-day running of prisons.

➤ **Health psychologists** assess people's attitudes, behaviour and thinking about health and illness. They work with other health professionals to help in communication with patients, and investigate how people's beliefs may affect their treatment.

➤ **Neurophysiologists** try to understand the relationship between the brain and psychological processes. They work towards the rehabilitation of patients who have suffered brain injuries, or perhaps have had their brain function affected by conditions such as strokes. They may be employed in the NHS or in the private sector.

➤ **Occupational or industrial psychologists** advise firms on the recruitment and training of staff in organisations and on improving the working environment.

➤ **Sport psychologists** work in competitive sport and recreation, increasing awareness of the relationship between the mind and physical performance.

Working outside psychology

Even if you don't want to become a psychologist, you might use some of your psychology skills in your chosen career. Your understanding of individual and group behaviour will be especially valued in counselling, social work, human resources, sales, marketing, careers guidance, and general administration and management. Equally you will have research and data management skills and the ability to think logically which could be of use in careers in IT and the financial sector.

Sources of information

British Psychological Society (BPS)
www.bps.org.uk

British Association of Counselling and Psychotherapy
www.bacp.co.uk

Careers in Psychology
www.careersinpsychology.co.uk

> *'It's not enough just liking people as you may deal with people you don't like and you'll have to put your own feelings aside.'*
> Christine, BSc psychology undergraduate

RELIGIOUS STUDIES

Religious studies gives you an understanding of world religions, philosophy and ethics. You certainly don't need to be religious to study it and students of any or no faith at all will find it an extremely challenging subject. You will study one religion in depth and find out how religious beliefs have influenced the world we live in, including through law and politics. You will gain useful debating, discussion and research skills.

What do you study?

The topics listed give an idea of what could be covered. The exact content of specifications differs according to exam boards. You will need to check with your school or college about the exact options available to you.

The new specifications encourage you to develop your interest in religion and belief and relate it to the wider world, to develop an understanding and appreciation of religious thought and its contribution to individuals, communities and societies, and you will undertake a specialist study of one world religion.

➢ **Philosophy of religion** – this covers the philosophical arguments about the existence of God, starting from ancient philosophical arguments. It includes studying arguments for the existence of non-existence of God, the nature of God, the problem of evil and suffering, the nature of the soul, mind and body, self and life after death, religious experiences, religious language, miracles and atheism.

➢ **Ethics of religion** – this covers the relationship between morality and religion and the various ethical dilemmas people face. It includes studying ethical theories, ethical language and thought, issues of human life and death, issues of animal life and death, free will and moral responsibility, conscience, sexual ethics and the influence on ethical thought of developments in religious beliefs. You will apply ethical theory to issues in the world today.

Throughout these topics examples are drawn on from world religions, the media and contemporary society. You will consider scholarly contributions to these topics such as those from Bentham and Kant.

➢ **Specialist study of one world religion**: Buddhism, Christianity, Hinduism, Islam or Judaism.

In your chosen religion you will examine the different aspects of the religion and how it has developed:

- sources of wisdom and authority, such as the main texts of the religion

- religious beliefs, values and teachings, their interconnections and how they vary historically and in the world today
- practices which shape and express religious identity, and how these vary within a tradition
- self, death and the afterlife
- good conduct and key moral principles
- the relationship between religion and society.

It is not essential to have studied GCSE religious studies in order to take the A level – the examination boards clearly state that the course is intended to be accessible to students of any background. A good grade in GCSE English or history would indicate that you could cope well with the research and writing involved.

Subject combinations

Religious studies can be combined with almost any other subject. If you are considering religious studies at a higher level, you might consider studying an ancient language, classical civilisation or philosophy. More common combinations are history, sociology, drama, English literature, media studies, psychology and business studies.

Higher education options

It is not essential to have an A level in religious studies in order to study it at a higher level, but normally at least one essay-based subject is required.

Degree-level study

Religious studies generally examines religion as a worldwide phenomenon. It includes the study of the major world religions. You study the history of the religions, the moral issues that they address, and their place in the world today. Theology or divinity degrees concentrate on Christianity. You might learn Biblical Hebrew and/or New Testament Greek, and the emphasis is on the study of Christianity from its inception to the present day. This includes an examination of its cultural, ethical, philosophical and historical developments. Biblical studies deals specifically with the Bible, its content and the changing approaches to it over the centuries. Specialised courses are available in Islamic studies and Jewish studies.

Degree subject combinations

There are an increasing number of degrees combining religious studies with related subjects such as religion, philosophy and ethics; religion, ethics and society; or theology and religious studies. Also there is the combination of theology with world religions.

There are many joint degree courses available and you can combine theology or religious studies with most subjects. The most popular options are history, English, philosophy, sociology or languages. You could also combine with related subjects like church history.

Specialist degrees such as Islamic studies can be combined with Arabic and Jewish studies can be combined with Hebrew.

Other higher education qualifications

There are foundation degrees in ministerial theology, theology, and Christian theology and practice (for those wishing to work in the church).

There are no HNDs or HNCs available but many universities and colleges, including theological colleges, run diploma and certificate courses of various kinds, some of them part time or as evening classes. Some offer courses for the University of Cambridge Certificate in Religious Studies and many run their own courses, most of which are intended for those planning a career in the Christian ministry.

Relevance to other subjects?

There are many other degree courses you could consider with a religious studies A level, such as American studies, combined studies, English, history, law, philosophy, politics, psychology, social science and teaching. It is acceptable as an entry qualification for any humanities or social science course. Anthropology, which involves looking at human culture in all its forms, including the role of religion and ritual in developed as well as 'primitive' societies, would be particularly enhanced by a knowledge of religion and religious behaviour.

Important advice

Make sure you research degree programmes carefully as some degrees just focus on one or two religions, whereas others cover many different faiths or broader issues. Some courses offer the opportunity to study abroad at another university or to study a particular religion during the summer vacation, for example in India. You should make sure the course matches your interests. If you are not sure whether you want to do your whole degree in religious studies, you might want to look at courses where you can combine subjects or have the option to add to or change your subjects after the first year.

Future careers

After A levels

Religious studies A level is regarded by many employers as a reliable academic qualification. It suggests that you can communicate your ideas clearly and effectively and have strong written and verbal skills. It is a useful additional A level for many careers and would be acceptable for many jobs and apprenticeships including business and administration, legal services, retail, the Armed Forces and social care.

After a degree

Working in religious studies

There are a number of careers related to religious studies, most requiring some further training:

➢ **teaching religious studies in schools** – there are some openings for religious studies teachers in primary and secondary schools; to teach in state schools you must undertake further training to gain QTS (Qualified Teacher Status). Opportunities may be available to teach in colleges and universities.

➢ **ordained ministry or other full-time careers in the church** – this requires additional training over a number of years. You must have total commitment and dedication.

➢ **museum work** – you might be able to use your knowledge of different religious traditions and their historical development by becoming a specialist in the field of religious artefacts. A postgraduate qualification would help in this type of work.

➢ **research and teaching in universities** – staff in universities usually carry out research as well as teaching, and there may be opportunities as research assistants. You could be involved in researching anything from ancient Hindu traditions to the modern evangelical movement in the USA.

Working outside religious studies

Only a few graduates in religious studies go on to a career with a religious organisation. Most use their skills in other areas such as caring professions and charity or advice and counselling work. Remember that a large proportion of graduate jobs are open to graduates in any subject, so if you are interested in a religious studies degree, don't worry about it being a disadvantage to you in the future. The critical thinking skills and the understanding of people developed in a religious studies degree will help you at many levels in the world of work from business and accountancy, to law, HR, retail or travel and tourism.

Sources of information

www.reonline.org.uk

www.rsrevision.com

'I enjoyed my degree; it taught me how to think logically, research effectively and gave me an understanding of people. It was no problem getting my first graduate job.'
Brian, HR manager, with a degree in theology

SOCIOLOGY

Sociology is concerned with why society works in the way that it does, and the extent to which our behaviour and even our opportunities can be shaped by our social class, age, gender, disability and race. It questions the society in which we live in order to understand the relationship between individuals and institutions such as the education system, religion and the mass media. Each of us is a member of a variety of social groups. In A level sociology you are required to take a step back from your personal interpretation of the world and look at how you too may have been influenced or shaped by these groups. You'll study key concepts such as power, gender, ethnicity and culture, as well as mass media, education, crime, deviance and religion.

What do you study?

The topics listed give an idea of what could be covered. The exact content of specifications differs according to exam boards. You will need to check with your school or college about the exact options available to you.

The new specifications are arranged under two core themes:

- **socialisation, culture and identity**
- **social differentiation, power and stratification.**

There is also a greater emphasis on working with qualitative and quantitative data as well as research methods.

➢ **Methods** – how sociologists obtain information about society; the advantages and disadvantages of different methods of research; quantitative and qualitative methods of research; research design: sources of data, including questionnaires, interviews, participant and non-participant observation, experiments, documents and official statistics; the distinction between primary and secondary data, and between quantitative and qualitative data.

➢ **Social differentiation and stratification** – social inequality and difference, social class, ethnicity, gender, disability and age; how these affect an individual's access to work, wealth, education and other social resources. The socialisation process and the role of the agencies of socialisation; the problems of defining and measuring social class; occupation, gender and social class; the nature, extent and significance of patterns of social mobility.

➢ **Sociology of youth** – key concepts and the social construction of youth, the role of youth culture/subcultures in society, the relationship between youth and subculture and the experience of young people in education.

➢ **The family** – types of family structure and how families differ across social groups; marriage, divorce and gender roles; the position of children in the family and wider society. Demographic trends in the UK: birth rates, death rates, family size, life expectancy, ageing population, migration and globalisation.

➢ **Education** – the relationship between social class, social mobility and education; how 'culture' is passed on through education; educational institutions; the curriculum; educational achievement between genders and different ethnic groups.

➢ **Culture and identity** – different types of culture within society such as subculture, mass culture, popular culture and global culture. How our sense of the 'self', identity and difference as both socially caused and socially constructed. The relationship of identity to age, disability, ethnicity, gender, nationality, sexuality and social class in contemporary society.

➢ **Deviance and control** – how to define antisocial behaviour; the possible causes and outcomes of crime; how social order and control are achieved through laws and social 'norms' (generally agreed codes of behaviour); the social distribution of crime and deviance by ethnicity, gender and social class, including recent patterns and trends in crime; globalisation and crime in contemporary society; the media and crime; green crime; human rights and state crimes, crime control, surveillance, prevention and punishment, victims, and the role of the criminal justice system and other agencies.

➢ **Health** – provision of, and access to, healthcare in contemporary society and inequalities in distribution. The role of medicine, the health professions, the welfare state and the globalised health industry.

➢ **Work, welfare and poverty** – definitions of poverty and the reasons for its continuation; distribution of wealth and income; poverty and exclusion; organisation and control of the labour process, including the division of labour, the role of technology, skill and de-skilling. The significance of work and worklessness for people's lives and life chances, including the effects of globalisation.

➢ **The media** – how new media reflects or influences culture and ideas; ownership and control of the media; selection and presentation of news and information. How the mass media presents age, social class and ethnicity; the media, globalisation and popular culture; media representations of age, social class, ethnicity, gender, sexuality and disability; the relationship between the media, their content and presentation, and audiences.

> **Globalisation and the digital social world** – developments in digital communication in a globalised society, such as social media and the impact of digital forms of communication on people's identities, relationships and on social inequalities. The impact of digital media and communication on culture, and the positive and negative impacts of digital forms of communication.

> **Global sociology** – development and underdevelopment and global inequality; globalisation and its influence on the cultural, political and economic relationships between societies; the role of transnational corporations, non-governmental organisations and international agencies in local and global strategies for development; development in relation to aid and trade, industrialisation, urbanisation, the environment, and war and conflict; employment, education, health, demographic change and gender as aspects of development.

> **Beliefs in society** – the role of religion in society (as a conservative influence or agent of change); religious institutions and how they are changing; religions in a multicultural society: secularisation; New Age movements.

You don't need GCSE sociology to take the A level, but it will obviously help you with your further studies. You will need a good pass at GCSE English as the course and exam involve essay writing. Maths will also be important as there is a lot of data and statistics to analyse.

The course contains a lot of reading, essay writing and class discussion. DVDs, newspaper articles and the web are used to show how sociology relates to the world around us. You may go on visits, for example to the public gallery of a court to see a variety of different cases. You may hear speakers such as the police or someone from a different religion talking about how it affects their life and how they live.

Subject combinations

Sociology could combine with and complement subjects such as politics, psychology or economics and would also combine well with arts subjects. If you are considering a BSc in sociology or social sciences, it would be a good idea to combine sociology A level with a more numerate/quantitative subject such as maths, statistics or computer science or consider taking Core Maths. You will need at least GCSE maths at a good grade to cope with the research and statistics involved in the course.

Higher education options

It is not necessary to have studied A level sociology in order to study it at university, although the background knowledge provided by your A level would certainly help with the first year of your degree.

Degree-level study

A degree in sociology may be a BA or BSc. In some cases this indicates whether the approach is more on the arts or the science (specifically quantitative) side. This means you should check the content of each course carefully before applying.

The first year of a sociology degree course covers some of the topics you will already have looked at during your A level studies, but in much more depth. Many first-year courses are quite broad, offering you a general introduction to the social sciences and covering subjects such as sociological theories; crime and deviance; popular culture and the media; gender, race and sexuality; research methods; and globalisation. They may include options in the study of social policy, psychology, economics, politics and languages.

In your second and third years, you will be able to specialise in areas that particularly interest you, for example, crime, community and culture, sociology of the media, music and society or understanding popular culture,

Degree subject combinations

You can combine sociology with many subjects, but the most widely available are history, politics, economics and English. There are combinations in related areas such as psychology, criminology and social policy.

Other higher education qualifications

There are foundation degrees in social sciences and sociology with psychology. There are related degrees in public services, criminology and psychology, criminology and criminal justice, police and criminology, community health and wellbeing, community leadership, community mental health, social care, youth and community justice, social policy, health and housing, and in children, young people and families.

HND and HNC courses are available in public services, in working with children and families, public and community services and health and social care management.

Relevance to other subjects?

One of the most popular alternatives is to take a degree in social work, and to qualify as a social worker. (N.B. It is possible to take a postgraduate qualification for social work training after other degree subjects.) For all social work courses you will need a DBS criminal record check.

Other popular options are public services management, community studies and counselling degrees. You could also look at criminology or criminal justice, politics, housing studies, health and social welfare, development studies, economics, geography and history.

Important advice

For entry to teaching, there are social science PGCE courses as well as postgraduate school training places, which are specific to the 14 to 19 teaching age groups. The courses include sociology but may ask for another subject specialism such as history, religious education, economics or psychology. You might consider a joint degree in sociology and another subject, if you want to study sociology without jeopardising your chances of going into teaching later on. It is important to check the acceptability of your intended degree carefully with postgraduate teacher training providers before you start your degree course. Don't forget that for teaching in secondary schools you will need GCSE maths and English at grade C or above (or equivalent grades with the revised GCSEs).

Future careers

After A levels

Employers will value your understanding of human social behaviour as well as your research skills. Career opportunities include working for the government, market research, human resources, the police or prison service. If you want to go into social work later on, you could build up experience by working in a social services support job, e.g. as a care assistant. There are apprenticeships in health and social care and Higher Apprenticeships in care leadership and management and HR management.

After a degree

Working in sociology

➤ **Social researcher** – working for market research organisations, charities, educational organisations, local or national government; may require getting further qualifications in information management or social research methods.

➤ **Social worker** – supporting and advising people who experience health or social problems within the community; you would need to do postgraduate study for this unless qualification was included in your first degree.

➤ **Teacher** – in a school or college, for which you would need to undertake further training to gain QTS (Qualified Teacher Status). See the important advice section for more information.

➤ **Administrator** – for local government in departments such as education, housing or social services, central government or charities.

➤ **Counsellor, welfare worker or community advice worker** – working in a variety of settings, providing support and advice to a range of clients. You would need further training.

Working outside sociology

You will have developed valuable research skills as well as knowledge of how society works, which would be useful in a range of careers from advertising, marketing and human resources through to the emergency services.

Sources of information

The Social Research Association
www.the-sra.org.uk

British Sociological Association
www.britsoc.co.uk

Skills for Care
www.skillsforcare.org.uk

www.sociology.org.uk

> *'I enjoy sociology because it is relevant to everyday life. You can see the concepts involved in sociology every day, which makes it interesting.'*
> Andrew, 16, studying sociology, English, psychology and law

USEFUL INFORMATION

Joint Council for Qualifications (publish national exam results)
www.jcq.org.uk

AQA
www.aqa.org.uk

Cambridge Pre-U
www.cie.org.uk

CCEA
www.ccea.org.uk

International Baccalaureate Organisation
www.ibo.org

OCR
www.ocr.org.uk

Pearson Edexcel
http://qualifications.pearson.com/en/home.html

Scottish Baccalaureate
www.sqa.org.uk/baccalaureates

Welsh Baccalaureate
www.welshbaccalaureate.org.uk

WJEC
www.wjec.co.uk

What do graduates do?
http://www.hecsu.ac.uk/current_projects_what_do_graduates_do.htm